WILLIAM LEITH has worked ⸺ writer at the *Independent on Sunday*, ⸺ *Sunday* and the *Observer*. His writing spans a wide range of subjects, from food to celebrity, cosmetic surgery, fashion and film. He has written about kings in Africa, political tension in Palestine, gold mining in the Klondike, Hollywood film directors, diet gurus and the death of James Dean. He is the author of three previous books: *The Hungry Years*, *Bits of Me Are Falling Apart* and *The Trick*.

THE CUT
THAT
WOULDN'T
HEAL

Finding My Father

WILLIAM LEITH

BLOOMSBURY PUBLISHING

LONDON · OXFORD · NEW YORK · NEW DELHI · SYDNEY

BLOOMSBURY PUBLISHING
Bloomsbury Publishing Plc
50 Bedford Square, London, WC1B 3DP, UK
29 Earlsfort Terrace, Dublin 2, Ireland

BLOOMSBURY, BLOOMSBURY PUBLISHING and the Diana logo are
trademarks of Bloomsbury Publishing Plc

First published in Great Britain 2022
This edition published 2023

A catalogue record for this book is available from the British Library

ISBN: HB: 978-1-5266-2378-2; PB: 978-1-5266-2379-9;
EBOOK: 978-1-5266-2368-3; EPDF: 978-1-5266-4399-5

2 4 6 8 10 9 7 5 3 1

Typeset by Newgen KnowledgeWorks Pvt. Ltd., Chennai, India
Printed and bound in Great Britain by CPI Group (UK) Ltd, Croydon CR0 4YY

To find out more about our authors and books visit www.bloomsbury.com
and sign up for our newsletters

To Susan

Seconds

Ten seconds before my father's death, I have a premonition – that the breath he is taking will be his last.

Of course, I've had these premonitions before. As he breathes out, I watch and listen, and I hold my own breath, and I wait for him to breathe in again. And every time I think he won't, but he does. It's getting harder, but he does, as he is doing now.

That's the good part – the intake of air. Then comes the terrifying part, when the air, the carbon dioxide I suppose, comes back out. Then there's a gap, followed by another uphill climb, another attempt on the summit.

I urge him on.

Come on! You can do it! He is eighty-six.

We're in a ward, in a hospital, eight beds, eight very old men. It's 9.35 on a black January evening. I'm supposed to leave the ward in twenty-five minutes. But I can't imagine my father will be alive in twenty-five minutes. That would be a lease of life – a bonus. I want it but I don't want it. I want to be with him when he dies. But I don't want to be with him when he dies. But, of course, I do. My brain is confused; I'm entering a period of shock.

We were never close, by the way. This, these last few days, is the closest we've been for years, maybe decades. Since the weekend in Montreal in '79, I keep thinking, and then that time in Nova Scotia for – what, three weeks? Driving by the side of the big lake. Since then I've *seen* him a lot – it's not that bad – but we've never talked much.

He stopped talking three days ago. And then came the days of the hand signals. I'd talk and he'd move his hands in response. Now I just talk. I'm pretty sure he can hear me, that it matters, that I matter to him, a very self-centred thing to think. I am very self-centred.

But these last few days have made me think how different things might have been. I might have been different, might have been closer to my father, if—

Oh, come on! What about that last time I bumped into him in town? When we didn't go to a cafe, didn't have a cup of coffee? Why did he not want to, I keep thinking – but of course he had his reasons, must have had his reasons. He said he wanted to do this and that on his own, had made a plan, wanted to stick to the plan.

Well, fine.

Not many more chances, I thought even then. Not many more chances to sit down and have a chat. Father and son, chatting away. But he had his plan. So it never happened.

One day, fifty days ago, I was sitting on a bench by the sea, and my phone went. And now, fifty days later, here we are. I'm talking. But I don't know what to say. And he can't say anything. All he can do is breathe.

So really this idea – the idea that things might have been different – is probably just a deathbed fantasy. He was always disappearing, my father, always living in different countries, and travelling to yet more countries. Superficially it seemed to make sense – he was a professor or a visiting professor here or there, Germany or Holland, say, and he worked for UNESCO in Paris. Hence the travel – to Africa, to the Middle East, to Latin America, often to dictatorships or Communist countries. As a teenager, I met him in Swiss and German hotels. Twice he moved to Canada.

I liked him.

He once said to my mother, in jest, that whenever he went somewhere, there was always some kind of coup or uprising. Not Canada or Holland, obviously. But—

He was a psychologist.

Is a psychologist.

He moved back to England after I left home. Soon after that, something odd happened. One day I found him in his room, his study I suppose, very unusual for the door to be open, and he was looking at all these dictionaries – Dutch, German, Swedish – and taking notes. It was his hobby, his passion in life, he said. Tracking words across different languages. And this took my breath away. Because it was my hobby too. As a student, I would smoke weed and read dictionaries for hours.

That thing of being slumped, surrounded by dictionaries!

Hey, I said to my father – I do the exact same thing. After that, we would buy each other books on linguistics.

So here we are. He cut his leg, and the cut wouldn't heal. And then, fifty days ago, I was sitting on a bench by the sea, and my phone went. It's all happened so slowly, and so fast. It goes round and round in my mind. A cut that won't heal, a collapse, a trip to the hospital, a course of powerful antibiotics. He was supposed to leave hospital after one day. But he did not leave. He stayed.

Now he can barely suck air into his lungs. I'm watching his face, his chest. He's going to try to take another breath. He's like a weightlifter.

Come on! Come on!

Today we've been – I've been – talking about various things. His love of languages, how he inspired me, which I suppose he must have done. I remember when he moved to Utrecht for a while and could actually pronounce Dutch words. I was maybe twelve. He'd been in Germany before that, and told me how Dutch was close to German and also Flemish and Frisian, which some people still speak.

He studied Old Norse. The last book I bought him was *Through the Language Glass*, by Guy Deutscher.

I've been telling him, over and over, what an inspiration he has been to me, how much I loved him, dropping in memories here and there – all in the tones of a talk-show host. Meanwhile he declines.

There's a barrier between my performance, on the one hand, and my feelings. My feelings, too dangerous to explore, are on the other side of the barrier.

He was always very tolerant. I would be drunk or high, and he never seemed to mind. Once I met him in the kitchen, one of those odd times we were in the same house. I must have been in my twenties, I'd been smoking weed, was high, and he made me a drink, and I actually bit into the glass, had glass and blood in my mouth, and he said, you OK, and I said, yes, I just bit the glass, but I think I'm OK. And that was that. I spat the shards of glass out of my mouth, and then we watched a late-night film.

He loved Westerns and cop shows. Wherever he went, he left a pile of thrillers.

The deal in this hospital is that every so often I ask my father if he wants morphine, and if he does, he taps his chest. We have a system. If he does want morphine, I go to find a nurse, and there's a procedure to be followed – signatures, clipboards, a five-minute wait. Then he gets a morphine injection. Then he's drowsy for a bit, and then he perks up.

This time, though, he hasn't perked up quite as much. The doctors will give him drugs to mask his symptoms. But they no longer allow him drugs to treat his symptoms. In terms of pharmacology, this can be a subtle distinction. In terms of the value of his life, it's a sad diminishment. A loss of prestige. He breathes in, and out. I look at him. He is almost eighty-seven. I am fifty-three. He begins to breathe in. That's when I get my premonition.

And then something unexpected happens. I have an urge to stand up, to walk away from my father's bedside. Driven by something – fear, an acute stab of self-centredness perhaps – I stand up and start to walk, first one step and then two, away from my father.

He has less than ten seconds to live.

Fifty Days Ago

Even though my career in journalism is on the slide, partly because journalism itself is on the slide, I'm asked to pose for a picture in a magazine.

The photographer asks me to sit on a bench by the sea. Above me is some kind of Victorian shelter. It's a cold day in November.

The last time I was here, in almost this exact spot, somebody took my picture to illustrate another article I was writing. The article was about the passage of time. My point was that, as you get older, time passes more quickly – or rather, it *seems* to pass more quickly. Also, your brain wants you to think time is speeding up. When you reach a certain age – around fifty – your perception of time will enter a new phase. You'll feel like your life is slipping away. This reminds you to act, to achieve something before it gets too late.

In the photograph I was looking into the sky, with a high grey sea behind me. I looked puzzled and scruffy.

Today, I look better. I'm wearing a short navy blue coat I bought in a sale, black needlecord trousers, and trainers by Vans. The photographer asked me to bring a scarf, which I'm wearing reluctantly. I'm not a scarf person. But he thinks it will look good by providing contrast, and I don't want to argue.

He clicks away. He's trying to reconcile the person he sees – me, in a coat and scarf – with the person he sees in his mind's eye: in other words the person he wants to see, I would guess a troubled person, a person with problems.

The article I'm writing is about giving up alcohol. So really, I'm posing, here on this bench, as my former self – the drinker, the alcoholic. I pose with and without a beer glass, which is about two-thirds full of the actual poison. My name is William Leith, I'm thinking, and I'm an alcoholic. At this particular time, I'm 324 days sober. The publication of the article will mark a year's sobriety – if I get there.

A mile away, out at sea, there is a wind farm. White stalks with propellers. But not exactly propellers, are they, because they do not propel. There must be another word. Sometimes I can see the stalks through the mist, and sometimes also the things that are not propellers.

What was it my father said the other day? That wind farms don't work, and actually make things worse, for a number of reasons. They may look virtuous, he said, but they are not. Listening to this, I felt a tiny stab of rage.

I should tell him about the Wright brothers, I thought, but did not.

As the photographer clicks away, I try to remember why I became an alcoholic. The drinking started in boarding school, because I felt bad about not being at home, and also bad about home itself, home being different now, never the same again. All these years later, thinking these thoughts makes me uncomfortable; a cloud of pre-tears rises a notch in the space behind my eyes.

Still I, the new me, must not run away from these memories – about how I wanted to escape, not exactly from school but from my life, and how drink was the obvious way, the ticket away from difficult feelings, of not being good enough, not clever enough, not successful enough, and later of not being a committed partner, not being strong enough to be a committed partner, not being all those things you're supposed to be in adult life, so I kept drinking, kept buying the ticket, which made things better and then worse, and then a lot worse, and I began to lie to people, and I began to lie to myself, and things went downhill from there.

I self-sabotaged.

Sabotage, from the French word *sabot*, a wooden shoe – sabotage is something perpetrated by people with wooden shoes, the working class in other words, who would hurt their bosses by damaging the factory they worked in. Self-sabotage, therefore, is damaging the factory of yourself.

I wonder if that's how he sees me, this photographer, as the sort of person who damages his own factory.

Did I try to damage myself?

The photographer tells me to move my chin and eyes this way and that. So I move my chin and eyes. Offshore, I can see the white things and the spinning things through the mist. What are they called? They look like sculptures.

My phone buzzes in my pocket. When I look at the missed call, the word on the screen is 'Parents'.

The Prognosis is Unmentionable

There's never been a time in my life when I could honestly say that my father was 'well' – although sometimes I might have said it for the sake of form. Physically, he's never been well. As a child he had a bad case of rheumatic fever and almost died; the illness left him with a permanently damaged heart. As a young man, he had stomach ulcers so disastrously that part of his stomach had to be removed. For years, he vomited and spat blood. Since then, he's had weight problems (too fat), and sleeping problems. Also, he keeps passing out.

He has never exercised. As a boy, he never willingly played any sport. When forced, he would stand still on the field, avoiding the ball. In middle age, he would walk through an airport, or across a car park, but would not 'go on a walk'. In his sixties, my mother would coax him to join her on short walks, to get out of the car and pick berries, maybe. He was not a beach person. He disliked the outdoors.

I've talked to him about it. He rarely replies. He just looks at me. The look of pity. What a dumb question.

About twenty years ago, I asked him why he didn't hike, or run; he stared me down, and said, in his very precise voice, 'Because I don't want to.'

'Why?'

'Why do I need to know why I don't want to do something?'

'Um.'

'Change the subject.'

'You could play tennis.'

At this, he replied with the most withering snort of contempt I've ever experienced. And that was that. Connection over.

I've often tried to work out why he hated exercise. I came up with this: he must have never had a rush of endorphins. For various reasons (knee, ankle) I don't run. But I do hike; I do experience the 'walker's high' after a couple of miles. A mild opiate combined with a mild stimulant: perfect. Also: the more often you walk, the sooner the high arrives on each walk, and the longer it persists. To establish this process, your body must give you a small endorphin reward for a small walk, which makes you curious: do I get a bigger reward for a longer walk?

Yes, I do.

But I don't think my father's body gives him this early signal at all. So he's never been physically curious. He must think that the rest of us, going on our walks, are just grimly putting one foot in front of the other, for hours on end, feeling as flat as he does when he gets out of the car and walks the short distance to the blackberry area, wondering how much of this he'll need to endure before he can get back to his books.

I wish I'd asked better questions when I had the chance. But now the subject is closed.

My father's health peaked in middle age – in his fifties, after he quit smoking, but before he started to drink. I mean, obviously he drank. But then he started to *drink*. He eats moderately bad food. Not the worst. A lot of smoked meat. Tinned Polish pork, bacon, frankfurters, and something he calls 'Dutch boiling sausage'. That's a subject we have bonded on – pork sausages. Bratwurst, bockwurst, 'Milano' salami, *saucisson sec*, and those Danish sausages called *polser*, which are not quite the same as frankfurters, but very close. He likes certain types of mustard – German *Senf*, the word originating from the Altdeutsch *sinapaz*, which I think describes the mustard-seed plant. He eats sauerkraut, which is good, but dislikes green vegetables. He is unable to digest milk – a legacy of the partial gastrectomy – so he avoids dairy, which might be a good thing.

Once or twice in middle age, he says, he collapsed, did not totally lose consciousness, and was pronounced healthy in the emergency room. The collapses were a mystery. For these details, we rely on his own account, because he was living alone, in a house in some woods in Nova Scotia. More recently, he's been collapsing a lot. He faints, and then lies down, and my mother brings him what has become the unquestioned remedy – a stiff drink.

He *drinks*. Quite a lot. Mostly spirits.

Also, if this is relevant, quite a range of spirits. Clear ones, green ones, brown ones, reddish ones.

For at least a decade, he's been taking warfarin, a blood-thinning, or, to be more accurate, an anticoagulant drug. This is because of his damaged heart. His left atrium (I think) fibrillates, so it can't push the blood into his left ventricle (I think); blood therefore pools in and around the valves (I think). But for the warfarin, clots would form around these valves, would block the heart, might travel anywhere, including the brain. The downside of having no damaging clots – no *thrombi*, Latin for lumps, derived from the Greek word for curds – is, of course, having no *healing* clots.

Banish the *thrombus malus* at your peril, you might say, because you're also getting rid of the *thrombus bonus*.

In any case, my father has a weekly blood test to check his INR, his international normalised ratio, which needs to be around 2.5, which means that, in certain laboratory conditions, it should take his blood 2.5 times longer to begin the clotting process than, say, mine. The INR is one of the things he will talk to me about. Recently, he thinks, his readings have not been making sense.

About five years ago, he cut his leg, and the cut didn't heal for weeks. Then about ten months ago, he cut his leg again – the oft-remarked (by my mother) incident with the Japanese man in the briar patch. This time the cut did not heal for months. More recently, he cut this same leg on the dishwasher, which was in the open position – a glancing cut, apparently not caused by a misplaced knife, but by the dishwasher door itself. A graze rather than a nick, then. An abrasion. (From the Latin *ab*, meaning off, and *radere*, to scrape.) And this abrasion, which did not heal, became infected.

The infection has been getting worse. Bacteria, feeding on the exposed tissue, have created a battleground. A nurse comes every few days to treat the disputed territory and renew the dressing. But in this anticoagulant place, the hoped-for scab will not form.

Today has brought terrible news. The bandage was removed. The infection is now out of control. The prognosis is unmentionable. My mother looked at the leg. She saw the leg. Which is why my phone buzzed, why my screen said 'Parents', why I am walking up the drive of what was, at times, and was not, at other, very different times, my childhood home.

A Bracing Walk

My mother is at the door. I enter, smiling or possibly grimacing, an unreadable expression on my face, and walk through the small hall and into the extended kitchen, where my father sits on a sofa. I still have my coat and scarf on, and I really hope my mother does not mention the scarf, because I dislike scarves, have disliked them for decades, ever since some key moment in childhood a therapist would take an expensive hour to identify.

'I like the scarf,' says my mother. 'Where did you get it?'

'I . . . don't know.'

I pull a chair up to the sofa. My father has two looks – sometimes pale and deathly, sometimes not. Today he looks pinkish and youthful, for his age anyway. He's eighty-six, but looks about seventy-six. Like a chubby Dirk Bogarde. He is wearing a checked shirt, a loose sweater, grey slacks, brown shoes. If I didn't know about the leg, I would think there was nothing much wrong with him.

We look at each other. His expression is *slightly* glazed.
'Well,' I say.

I look around the room. It is cluttered, with too much furniture, too many chairs. A framed Vermeer print hangs above the kitchen table, with two postcards of the same painting stuck between the frame and the glass, which for whatever reason makes me feel a tiny bit weepy. I keep an alternative view of the kitchen in my mind's eye, as it was when it was mostly empty, when my parents were thousands of miles away, and I would come here from boarding school on Sunday afternoons, on my own, having taken two buses. I'd sit here, in this exact spot, possibly on this exact chair, and then go upstairs and lie on my bed; if I timed it right, if I was lucky with buses, I could stay here more than an hour. Sometimes I would sort of fool myself into thinking that I was not alone, that somebody else might be in another room.

Oh how very sad. What a sad teenager I must have been.

When I got back to school I'd sign myself back in right next to where I'd signed myself out, the two signatures identical.

'Where've you been, Leith?'

'For a walk, sir. Seafront, sir.'

'A bracing walk.'

'Yes, sir.'

Now I talk to my father, haltingly at first, and then more fluently after the subject of wind farms has been broached. I have something prepared, an analogy: the Wright brothers. I will mention Orville Wright, dressed as a bird, jumping off the bridge, landing in the water.

My father says: 'I have darter.'

'What?'

He reaches for a file, opens it, pulls out a sheet of paper. On the paper are columns of numbers he has written, and a list of bullet points. He says 'darter' just as he says 'apparattus', which always makes me think of *Rattus rattus*, the black rat, and *Rattus norvegicus*, the brown rat.

'Darter' is 'data'. In the 1960s, he said 'row-bow' for 'robot'.

'It is possible', he says, 'that the planet is warming as a result of human action. It is also possible that it is warming for another reason, or other reason-suh.'

'Right.'

'Or that scientists mistakenly think it is warming.'

'Um . . .'

'Or that, yes, the planet is warming – but this warming is temporary, and not part of a *general trend*.'

For me, either you buy into the concept of climate change (I do, possibly for selfish reasons), or you are a troublemaker, a conspiracist, possibly a nutcase. For my father, a student of Karl Popper – *literally* a student of Karl Popper – another position, a third way, exists. Before you believe something is real (say, climate change), you must try to falsify it, in every way you can, and even when you're sure you can't falsify it, you must only accept it provisionally. In the 1970s, scientists thought they had plenty of reasons to believe that the planet was *cooling*, another position my father accepted only provisionally. He thinks I believe the earth is getting warmer because it's fashionable to do so, just as he thought I listened to progressive rock not because it was good, but because it was a way of signalling some sort of kinship with my peers. (He was right.) He also said Mozart was superior to Pink Floyd, and that this could be demonstrated mathematically.

But now I wonder. Perhaps, at last, he has left behind the world of Popperian falsification, and crossed into the land of crazy. That glazed look in his eyes.

Actually, no. He is presenting a cogent argument.

He says: 'Even if the wind were to blow all the time, exactly where the turbines are placed, even if those rotors were spinning every minute of every day—'

Turbines, I am thinking. Rotors, I am thinking. Damn!

I chip in: 'Yes, but my point was going to be, and this is crucial—'

'Don't say that.'

'OK. My point. Think of Orville Wright. Dressing up as a bird. And then what?'

My father says: 'Either something is self-evidently crucial, or it's not.'

He has fifty days to live.

The Occult World

My mother and I go on a walk, across a cricket field and around some tennis courts. A walk is where we can talk about my father without him overhearing, because obviously he never joins us on the walk. Usually on these walks I criticise him, and then my mother defends him ('He had such a terrible start in life'), but sometimes it goes the other way: I criticise him, and she tells me how his behaviour, around the time I was born, was extremely unusual and definitely shocking. This is one of the things I *must not mention* in front of him.

But what would I say, anyway? 'Why did you stop speaking to her when she got pregnant?' Or: 'Why did you not come to the nursing home when I was born?' Or, more generally: 'Why were you never *there*? And always *somewhere else*?'

Naturally, I could never say these things to him; it would mean a conveyance of emotion from me to him (terrifying), and possibly even from him to me (absolutely out of the question). To me, my father exists on a plane of rationality and secrecy, and that's the only existence I can imagine for him. His has always been an occult world, and my role (which has its advantages) has been to accept this fact and live with it.

Today, my mother needs to talk about the cut. 'It won't heal,' she says more than once. Her view is that, if the cut does not heal, my father will be overwhelmed by the infection; having seen the cut, she believes this will happen quite soon. I can't imagine how she will feel, when my father disappears for a final time.

Can't or won't?

I say: 'I think he should stop taking the warfarin.'

'But his heart!'

'OK, but think – it might be the best option. Thicken the blood until the cut heals . . . and then *thin* the blood again, to save the heart.'

I have a hypochondriac's command of medicine, a lucky dip of fear and confirmation bias.

We walk past the tennis courts, and along the shrubbery path that leads to the churchyard, where my mother's mother's ashes lie under a flat stone. Unusually, we do not go into the churchyard.

My mother asks me what I am writing about. Ten seconds later, she is saying: 'But you're *not* an alcoholic! You're the opposite of an alcoholic! How can you say you're an alcoholic when you don't even drink!'

'That's why I don't drink – *because* I'm an alcoholic!'

'Well, if you are, *why* . . . why must you tell the world? Why do you want to tell the world all the bad things about yourself?'

'I—'

'Just tell me that. Why?'

And now, because I believe it to be the truth, I say: 'I can't do anything else.'

Last Train to Clarksville

Over the next few days, perhaps sensing the speeding passage of time, the brevity of life, I try to spring into action. I try to write about my drinking, or rather to think about my drinking, to think about writing about my drinking. I have, I'm pretty sure, lost the urge to drink. How did that happen? Maybe because I simply stopped drinking.

Addiction is a learning process – a form of brainwashing. If you want it to stop, it's something you need to unlearn.

As Allen Carr famously said of smoking, it's smoking that makes you want to smoke. People who have never smoked don't feel nicotine withdrawal. This is the point Neil Casey makes in his book *The Nicotine Trick*. Nicotine, say Carr and Casey, creates a need for nicotine. You might even use it as an analogy for what critics of capitalism call rent-seeking behaviour – nicotine is the middleman who makes himself indispensable without adding any value.

So: smoking makes you want to smoke. Does drinking make you want to drink?

Yes. But there are complications, in both cases. For instance, nicotine withdrawal stretches time out, making it pass more slowly, and then, briefly, faster, when the withdrawal is relieved. For the smoker, a sixteen-hour day might feel like seventeen hours.

For the drinker, the first ten hours of the day will feel like eleven hours, but the next six will pass in two or three – or even less, if you're in the grip of late-stage alcoholism. I knew a guy who needed to be drunk all the time; for him, a day felt like a couple of hours of consciousness, followed by a blackout, which felt like no time at all. The blackout was the thing he was really seeking; he said he could bring it on by snorting lines of heroin.

But if drinking begets more drinking (and it does), does not-drinking make you not want to drink? It does. There is a hump to get over – the period after you stop drinking, but before the absence of alcohol makes you stop wanting to drink. To get over this hump, you must have an active desire to not-drink.

Not the fleeting mid-hangover desire drinkers experience every morning. But a powerful belief that sobriety is urgent, a necessity. Sobriety is a train leaving the station very soon, and you absolutely must catch that train; this is your one opportunity to escape a dreadful fate. The Last Train to Clarksville. (The song may not be about sobriety, but it is unquestionably about urgency.)

Urge, from the Latin *urgere*, to drive, or press, or push forward, all these words suggesting agency; you must *do* something, immediately, because the clock is ticking.

In any case, *something* gave me a powerful urge to stop drinking. I'd be interested to know what it was. Just as pertinent, of course, is the other question: what gave me such a powerful urge to drink in the first place – to drink, to drink more and more, and then to stumble, to fall.

Also: I must declutter my house. I want to give it a pleasant, airy feel, partly so that when my son's mother, from whom I seem to be estranged, visits me, she will – what?

She will want me again, *if* my house is uncluttered, *if* it is pleasant and airy.

I have been reading Marie Kondo, who says you must throw away 75 per cent of the stuff in your cupboards. And here's the weird thing – I can't. I am emotionally attached to things I don't want – a key mental illness of our affluent society. Also, I am emotionally distant from people I *do* want. Ditto. Is this true? And if it is, why? Why do I hang on to these broken, useless things? Why do I shut them away in cupboards, out of sight?

They are the unwanted shards of my past. Unwanted, but also wanted. I keep them under control. I am afraid to let them go. I imprison them. But that's not true. They imprison me.

So I open the door to the cupboard under my stairs. It's a full-sized door, behind which is a huge space. Part of my attraction to this house was the amount of storage capacity it has – or, as an estate agent might hatefully say, 'boasts'. Five large built-in cupboards, eight feet high and ten feet wide, some of them.

The door clicks open on its ball-bearing mechanism. Ker-click.

And now something is *pushing* from inside the cupboard, something that wants to get out. Some *things*. Many things. Things that feel animate, but are not, must not be. I feel suddenly sick, as if I've eaten too much monosodium glutamate – a condiment my father adores, by the way: a choice I can't understand – it makes my neck feel hot and bloated.

Which it does now.

I close the door.

Something I Couldn't See

A therapist once asked me when 'things' started to go wrong for me. And I have a stock answer: in the autumn of 1969, when I was nine, with the peeing thing. At the time, I couldn't understand the peeing thing. My father took me to the family doctor, who was posh, and old, who must have been born in about 1910; he had a Roman nose with a sharp break at the bridge, I imagine from boxing or rugby at some boarding school, and we sat there, in the surgery in his Georgian townhouse, and I tried to explain the peeing thing, and could not even begin.

It wasn't until I was middle-aged, and a therapist asked me to piece everything together, asked me to think about what *else* was happening in the autumn of 1969, that I began to see some clear shapes emerging from the murk.

But these days I cast my mind back even further, to a time before the peeing thing, before the sudden move to Canada in August 1968, and even before my father's earliest disappearances – to Berlin in the autumn of 1966, to Prague in 1967, to Bulgaria in 1968.

Did my neuroses, specifically my feeling that I *was not clever enough*, date back as far as 1966, when I was six, living in the house in Birmingham?

Possibly.

In 1966, my father was working at the University of Birmingham. This was before he started to disappear, at least in a physical sense, although he was absent and disconnected in other ways. Like, emotionally. At home, he was almost always in his study. If not, he needed to *get back* to his study as soon as possible. Then he'd shut the door, and remain in the study for several hours. I suppose there would be bathroom breaks. And sometimes he would make himself a sandwich. Ham with mustard and gherkin? He'd be in the kitchen, very briefly, then it was back to the study, the door closed, and after that you might not cross paths with him for a couple of days.

I never knocked on his door; the study, I understood, was out of bounds.

So. The cleverness thing. In the 1960s, my father was working on a project, a *system*, he called Programmed Learning. He wanted to understand what made facts and ideas stick in people's minds. First of all he tested people, for general intelligence and personality traits, and input all the data into a very early computer, a thing about the size of four or five fridges, battleship grey, with dials and switches and needle displays. He observed the steps people took to solve problems, how efficient they were, how easily they made their minds up about this or that, and how their minds could be changed. He fed punchcards into the grey machine. He asked the grey machine for answers. Then he wrote up the results and published them in psychology journals.

One day, he asked me if I would like to take some of his tests. How about an IQ test to start with? I would solve a series of problems, and then he would tell me how well I had done. In other words, how clever I was.

Before I go any further with this, I'd like to fill in some details about my social circle at the time. My father had two main friends – or maybe faculty colleagues would be a better term. Peter and David. Both physicists. My close friends were the sons of these men. Richard, Michael and Chris.

And Richard, Michael and Chris were smart kids.

To add context: David would win the Nobel Prize in Physics; Michael would, I think, become a rocket scientist (designing the nose-cones for space shuttles, if I'm right); Chris would discover a new type of lion – or, I suppose, a type of lion that had been there all along, but that was different in a way he would be the first to notice; Richard would win the Fields Medal for mathematics (there is no Nobel Prize for mathematics; the Fields is its equivalent). Chris would win the Queen's Medal for Bravery for facing down a rampaging elephant with his bare fists and saving a woman's life.

Richard would get two degrees from Cambridge; Michael would get one from Cambridge and one from

Harvard; Chris would get one from Oxford and one from Cambridge. At elementary school, I could tell that Richard was a better mathematician than our maths teacher. If you check out Simon Baron-Cohen's book *The Essential Difference*, about the 'extreme male brain', there's a chapter about a brilliant mathematician that he, Baron-Cohen, diagnoses with Asperger's syndrome. This is Richard.

So. My three childhood friends. Smart kids. And how did that make me feel? Well, it was definitely the start of something. I have always had an intense, even obsessive relationship with the cleverness of others. Even now – particularly now – when I talk about exceptionally clever people, my voice quavers and my eyes fill with tears.

Did I want to take my father's tests? Of course I did. And of course the idea terrified me.

He opened the door to his study. I stepped in. Looked around.

My memory of this event is stained with different versions of itself; I have often located the memory-document in my brain, told one or other version of the story, and replaced the document (now delicate with wear and tear) back in its cerebral filing cabinet.

Anyway, I walked into the study – definitely true. The study smelled of cigars. Again, true. My father had smoked cigarettes, starting in about 1943 or 1944. My mother forced him to quit twenty years later after the two famous studies by Richard Doll, linking cigarettes to cancer, had been generally accepted. (There was a time, in the 1950s and early 1960s, when people 'knew', but not in an absolute sense.) In any case, my father's solution was cigars – and, later, a pipe. ('He inhaled the cigars!' my mother would say later, and often.)

In the study, I took an age-appropriate IQ test – lots of small puzzles. I liked the puzzles, was quite good at solving them, and was given a score, although I don't remember it now. (Don't remember or won't remember?) Soon after this, on another day, I took a personality test. I turned out to be extroverted (a status that persisted until the age of about thirty-five, when it began to recede; now I live like a hermit most of the time). I was also rebellious, a divergent thinker, and I could tell right from wrong. All in all, I now think, a recipe for hard partying, dreaming the impossible dream, addiction, self-sabotage and guilt, with the small but very real possibility of living under a bridge.

But it was the puzzles that had hooked me. I asked my father if he would go through the puzzles one by one, especially the ones I had got wrong. I didn't want to get them wrong. I wanted to get them right.

My father: Look at this one. What do you see?
Me: A man. A car. The sun.
My father: What's wrong with the picture? What else
            do you see?
Me: The shadow? The shadow . . . is wrong.
My father: That's right. If the sun is *there*, the shadow
            should be *there*.
Me: I see! I see!

I could see it. I could see what was wrong with the picture. I liked these puzzles. I liked the tests.

I took more tests. Soon, I could always see what was wrong with the picture.

But there was something I couldn't see. I couldn't see what was wrong with always being able to see what was wrong with the picture.

Not a Comprehensive List

There are things I can talk to my father about, and things I can't talk to him about. For instance, I can talk to him about Stanley Kaplan, who studied the SAT test, which is very like an IQ test, in that it's supposed to be a way of measuring innate intelligence – supposed to be, but actually not. Kaplan discovered a way to game the test, by making a structural analysis of the questions. He saw how the questions worked. Once you can see how the questions work, you can pretty much get them all right. Malcolm Gladwell wrote a brilliant essay about it.

Another, related thing I can talk to my father about is the so-called Flynn effect – the fact that people, in general, seem to have higher IQs than they did in the past. For a while, this was a mystery. But not any more – the reason is that the world in general is becoming more and more like an IQ test. It's a series of puzzles and mathematical phenomena. In the modern world, everybody needs to analyse data, to understand sequences of numbers, to calculate compound interest, to see bias in themselves and others.

I can talk to my father about the movement of words and concepts across medieval Europe. So the Vikings took their word *ox*, meaning 'bull', to Iceland when they sailed across the Atlantic a thousand years ago – they still say *ox* in Iceland now. But then the Romans crept north, with their concept of *taurus*. And now, if you were in Sweden or Denmark, and you pointed at a bull, they would call it a *taur*, and if you said *ox*, they'd think you were harking back to ancient times. Actually, my father's family on his mother's side, the Mandersons, descend from the early Viking settlers, the guys with long blond hair and beards who would have attacked his family on his father's side, the Leiths; Mandersons would have hacked Leiths to death, about 800 years ago, and commandeered their cattle, and they might have referred to a bull as an *ox* or a *taur*, but it's hard to say which – timewise, that would have been right on the line.

Things I can't talk to my father about: the sudden, unexpected move to Canada, when I was eight; the fact that, for a time, he was bullied at school (lots of people were, for a time, but it marked him deeply, and he has locked it away); some details about his work in Communist Eastern Europe, the Middle East, Africa, Sri Lanka and South America; the sudden, unexpected moves to Germany and Holland; the second sudden, unexpected move to Canada; his sisters, who died in childhood; sex, bodily functions, his drinking. This is not a comprehensive list.

I'm Telling You to Color It In

A December morning in 1968. I'm eight, and I'm walking up a hill, on an icy path, in St John's, Newfoundland, with my father. He is wearing a black trilby. He is forty-one. St John's is the largest Irish city after Dublin. (Boston is bigger than both, but not so Irish.) My father is walking me to school for the first time. He has to see the principal because I'm in trouble.

The snow is three feet high on either side of us and sometimes higher, our path a sort of ice canyon. As we approach the school a gust of wind snatches my father's hat; we watch as it describes an arc against the white sky.

I know why I'm in trouble. It's because I don't fit in here, at St Michael and All Angels Elementary. Here, kids start school at six. Back home, I started at four, having learned to read at three. So I've been reading for five years. I read books all the time. Some of my classmates still can't read, can't multiply numbers, can't even add or subtract. A couple of boys have been held back a year – they're nine – and boy, do they hate me.

The trouble started on the first day. We were all given a maths workbook and a pencil, and told to do the sums in the book. Jeez, I thought – *thirty pages* of sums. I'd have to concentrate. It turned out the sums were fairly easy; there were just lots of them. When I was done I put my hand up and told the teacher I was finished.

He took the workbook and looked through it. He was angry. That was supposed to be several weeks' work!

I spent the rest of the lesson in disgrace, rubbing out my answers.

Then came reading and writing, art and more maths. In England, in the classroom with Richard and Chris, I'd felt like Gulliver in the land of giants. Now I was in Lilliput. In Lilliput, some of my classmates appreciated the fact that I could read whole books, that I could spell, that I could write little essays, that I knew the Latin names for mammals and birds, that I could add, subtract, multiply and divide. Most did not.

One autumn day, after class had finished, I picked up my school satchel, hung the strap on my shoulder, and walked out of the classroom and along the corridor and out of the front gate, and I walked around the side of the building, and there were some boys waiting there. I saw something in their faces, and as I stepped beyond the corner of the building, something doubled me up, a gut punch, a fist to the solar plexus, a perfect strike, and I fell backwards against the wall, and I slid down the wall, and looked up; it was Wayne Sullivan, one of the nine-year-olds, the one who had the most trouble reading.

I looked up, trying not to cry. Wayne Sullivan walked away. Then the other boys walked away, and then I got up and followed them down the path. They weren't looking at me.

I know I could have played things differently. When Wayne Sullivan, his pride having been hurt in some classroom exchange, had cursed at me, had I tried to hurt his pride even more? Possibly. Had I succeeded? Probably. Would I try again? Definitely. Would Wayne Sullivan be waiting for me, day after day, just around the corner from the school entrance? Yes, he would. Would he hit me again? Yes, he would.

Yes, I'm thinking, I would needle him, with nuanced expertise. This, more than the hitting, is something I have mostly scrubbed from my memory; these classroom moments exist as flickering shadows, degraded old newsreels, locked in a room I don't allow myself to enter.

For Christmas, our class teacher asked us to copy an illustration of Santa Claus; we were each given colouring pens and a piece of stiff white paper. My Santa looked fine. I even remembered to put in the white crescents to suggest the shine on the toecaps of his boots.

The teacher saw his chance, I guess is what happened. To make an example of me.

'One boy has not colored in Santa's boots properly.'

And: 'William, *everybody but you* has completed the assignment.'

And: 'But you did not.'

And: 'Will you please color in the boots?'

And: 'Now, please.'

And: 'I won't tell you again.'

I refused: 'It's to show the shine.'

'I don't care if "it's to show the shine". I just told you what to do.'

'But the *original picture* (titters from the class at my use of language) is not colored in . . .'

'But I'm *telling* you to color it in. Now! If you don't, I will take you to the principal! And you can explain to the principal why you will not do this simple thing. Like everybody else did!'

And now, eighteen hours later, I'm walking up the hill with my father, through the canyon of ice. I can see the main entrance ahead of me. I can see the corner of the building where Wayne Sullivan waited, where Wayne Sullivan will be waiting again.

The principal said that whatever opinion I had about the boots, about the crescents of white on the toecaps of the boots, did not matter. I had to do what the teacher told me to do. That was what mattered. And if I did not do what the teacher told me to do, he, the principal, would call my parents.

My father is a few feet ahead of me in the ice canyon. Here is the school. Here is the gust of wind. The trilby describes an arc against the white sky, and then falls on the white ground, and wheels across the surface of the snow.

I think: he will have to wade into the snow; he will fall over; he will get stuck; he will fall and get stuck and people will see him; people will see him and they will see me and they will *know*; but he might just carry on walking; he might just leave it; he's leaving it; thank God.

When we get inside the school, my father turns towards the principal's office. He looks at me briefly. But I keep on walking, towards the classroom.

A Normal Psychologist

At about the time the ice canyons began to melt, my mother cracked, her patience went, and we flew back to England. My father did not come with us.

My mother hadn't liked anything about moving to Canada – the suddenness of the move, the lack of preparation, the fact that people were living in our rental house when we arrived, the fact that these people did not want to leave, the fact that they did not leave, the fact that we had to live in a motel for weeks. The house, when we finally moved in, had very little furniture. The cooker didn't work properly. We had arrived in August; we left, without my father, in March.

I went to stay with my grandparents in Newcastle-upon-Tyne. My mother went to Sussex to look for a house. (My father had arranged a job in England, in the psychology department at the University of Sussex; he was expecting to start in September.)

No more funny business, said my mother. No more sudden moves. This is it. More than anything, she wanted a normal life, a normal house and garden; she wanted my father to be a normal psychologist.

I went to school, for two weeks, in Newcastle. To me, the kids here seemed rough and urban, and even poorer than my classmates in Canada. They probably didn't spit as much. In Canada, they loved to spit.

When my mother found a house in Sussex, she came to get me, and I went to another school for a few weeks. Here, the kids seemed to be obsessed with sex and nudity. They streaked. They stripped. They drew pictures of male and female sex organs. My mother believed it was the sexual revolution, which hadn't been happening in Birmingham, or St John's or Newcastle. It was only happening in a few places. Sussex, a few miles south of Swinging London, was one of them.

The 'B' Stream

So, said my therapist, what *else* was happening at that time?

Well, I said, my mother enrolled me in this private school. A very Victorian place. The school was over-subscribed; it must have been popular. There was a place for me, but only in the 'B' stream. And oh, said the headmaster, there was a test. Sort of an IQ test. So I took the test. Every question, every little puzzle, I could see what the examiners had in mind. This sequence of numbers was designed to give you the wrong impression. These shapes were trying to misdirect your attention. This shadow was pointing over here, rather than over there.

The 'B' stream was great. I loved the 'B' stream. We had a lot of our lessons with a woman called Miss Chesterton. I have a feeling there was tragedy in her past, something to do with the war. Also, she kept talking about Dulwich College, she had a real thing about Dulwich College. She was great, Miss Chesterton. She taught us about sperm, and I remember someone's hand going up, and the boy whose hand it was said: 'Samir has sperm!' There were seventeen boys in the 'B' stream, and a few of them were from the Middle East, one or two from Africa. English was not everybody's first language. Samir was a year ahead; he'd be ten or eleven; he boarded at the school, and was in the same dormitory as the boy.

In the meantime, my test was marked. I had performed amazingly well. Of course I had. I knew how the test worked. I'd been in the 'B' stream for three weeks. Now I had to be in the 'A' stream. I swapped with another boy, who was at the bottom of the 'A' stream – a popular boy, not clever but not stupid, who would take my place in the 'B' stream, who would sit in my desk, towards the back of the room, a sunny room with big sash windows.

The 'A' stream, on the other hand, was in a sunken room, lower than ground level; it was full of sharp, competitive boys, all white; the first time I walked into the class they were talking to each other in Latin – actually a sort of Latin slang. They used Latinised names for each other: Cookus, Ricardus. Compared to the boys in the 'B' stream, they were edgy and mean. One boy sold pictures of naked female breasts he'd cut out of glossy magazines – he snipped them up, and put them in envelopes. You got a certain number of breasts for a shilling.

I walked into the classroom, and something smashed into me from behind, and I was on the floor.

When I looked up, someone said: 'Watch where you're going, idiot.'

'Yeah, idiot!'

'Dumbo.'

'Gittus stupidus.'

That's what I told my therapist. I have a whole theory of bullying, by the way – how it works, how to deal with it. The thing is, nobody actually wants to know how it works, bullying. They really don't.

And then there was my father. He'd left Canada, and something weird had happened, he'd disappeared again, and this had caused him to fall out with the psychology department at Sussex. And now, having arrived in Sussex, he was furious. He did a lot of hissing and cursing. He could not stay in Sussex. That was out of the question. He needed to leave – right now! He'd had an argument with the dean, who was wearing a loud tie; my father had pulled the dean's tie, and then flicked it in his face, and said, 'You and your *stupid* tie!'

At home, I was uncomfortable.

At school, I would pee in the urinal, and then I'd walk towards the washbasins, and then I'd turn around and go back to the urinal, and try to squeeze out another pee. I'd run to the urinal between lessons, and then run back towards the classroom, and turn around, magnetised by the urinal. The smell of it! Rich, heady. There was moss or lichen growing in the grouting between the ancient concrete slabs, feeding, I suppose, on the urine, soaking up the urine.

In the end, one of my teachers noticed my odd comings and goings, my shifty manoeuvres. My parents were called. My father took me to the family doctor in Lewes, with his Roman nose, his Roman nose with a sharp break at the bridge, probably from boxing or rugby at school, a man who spoke without opening his mouth, like a ventriloquist.

'Why do you keep wanting to go to the lavatory?'

'I don't know.'

'Can you try to go less?'

'Yes.'

That was it. My father drove me to school. He did not talk about the peeing thing. People have said: why not? He was a psychologist – you'd think the peeing thing was exactly the sort of thing he'd want to talk about. But no.

We sat in the car, not talking about the peeing thing. I watched my father's hand on the gearstick, grinding through the gears. It was the closest we'd been for a long time; it was the closest we'd get for a long time.

Slightly More Pinched

I'm sitting on my sofa at home, writing on plain A4 paper on a clipboard, or rather, not writing yet, but poised to write, when my phone, which is charging in another room, begins to ring.

I've been trying to write about why I stopped drinking. I may never know why I stopped drinking. But if I could find out, this would be useful knowledge, and if I had this useful knowledge, I could do something with the knowledge, do something useful with my life.

I had my last drink eleven months ago, in the early hours of the morning. I think it might have been around 2 a.m. I wouldn't have described myself as drunk. I would have said I'd had a few drinks. But I was drunk. If I had tried to drive, or write, or give a talk in public, I'd have done these things badly. Feeling neither happy nor sad, I raised the glass and swallowed the booze. It was some kind of fruit punch.

At some point, I experienced a moment of clarity. But why? And when? When did I experience this moment? A moment is something *momentous*, something *with momentum.* Thinking this, I put down my clipboard, and my ballpoint pen, and stand up. The phone has stopped ringing.

But I check it anyway. The missed call is from 'Parents'.

I call back. It was my mother. My father, she says, needs to go to the doctor. He needs to have his regular blood test. But for some reason, she can't take him in. He no longer drives – has not driven for five years. One day about six years ago he found it very hard to back out of the drive. This was because another car was parked across the road. If you could see the spaces, the angles, you'd see it was an easy thing to do, to back out of the drive with a car on the other side of the road. But my father couldn't see it. That's when he started driving less. The next thing: his footwork, he said, was not as dextrous – can feet be dextrous? – as it had been. Yes, feet can be dextrous. *Dexter* just means 'right', as *sinister* means 'left'. In his early eighties, his feet had started to feel sinister to him. At the age of eighty-two, he stopped driving altogether. One day, he just decided to stop, and he hasn't driven since.

A memory comes to me, something I wasn't expecting: the last time my father drove me any significant distance, with just the two of us in the car. It was ten years ago. My friend Jonathan's father had died. *My* father drove me, us, to the crematorium, and then to the reception afterwards, a round trip of thirty or forty miles, and I felt very weird and disturbed by the whole thing. Not just sad, which was true, I was broken up when Jonathan's father died – actually traumatised; I'd known the guy as a kid, he was always around, and I felt like I knew how Jonathan must have felt, although of course I didn't, but I felt like I knew. And I felt terrible. And I also felt something else, some weird horribleness on top of the terribleness I already felt, because Jonathan was always seeing his father. Even in adulthood, his father would come to his house to watch sport on TV; they were always doing something together, which I must have envied. And at the reception, there I was with my father. And I was *never* with my father.

The reception was at Jonathan's parents' lovely house in the country. It was mostly in the garden, it being summer, and Jonathan's father was signally not there, but his golf shoes were, placed together, the heel of one shoe resting on top of the other, as if the old guy was standing there at the edge of the garden. That really broke me up, and I thought: I won't be this sad at my father's funeral.

My father was charming at the funeral, he was always charming in public, and when we got in the car and drove back, the charm continued, and in the car I felt the terribleness, and the horribleness. But I also felt that my father wanted to be charming, to *me*, for the first time in years.

Today he needs to catch the bus. Could I, his middle-aged son, meet him at the bus stop and walk with him to the surgery? Of course I could. I'd be glad to.

I'm also glad to take a break from thinking about how I *messed up my life*, or at least sort of messed it up. I can get it back – maybe. Write something – maybe. Is that why I stopped drinking? A last chance to be a success, rather than the other thing?

My father gets off the bus – he is using his wry smile, is being charming to two older men as they step off the bus, two very old men, all three are very old. He is tottering on his bad leg. He looks slightly older, slightly more pinched than when I last saw him. The distance to the surgery is 200 yards. We walk along together. He has forty-five days to live.

In the surgery we sit down next to each other, not saying anything, waiting for his name to be called.

And then, out of nothing, he takes my right hand, and places it next to his left hand; the two are almost identical, as has sometimes been remarked – although his is paler, with some liver spots. We turn our heads towards each other; he looks at me, right in the eye, and I look at him, and I purse my lips, and nod almost imperceptibly.

I keep wanting to ask him the same question: why did you keep disappearing? Or maybe: why did you *want* to keep disappearing? Why did you *need* to keep disappearing? Not that I haven't asked him before, and not that he hasn't answered me. He was meeting colleagues. Meeting other psychologists. German psychologists, Dutch psychologists, American and Canadian psychologists. And these psychologists, they would meet in out-of-the-way places. That was part of the job.

My father's name is called. He disappears for twenty minutes, and when he appears again, he totters across the waiting room, and I put him in a taxi, making sure to wave as the taxi pulls away. This is the last time I see him outside the house he lives in or the hospital he will die in.

He Looks Great

Watching my father wave – the outstretched hand, the weak smile as he is conveyed away – makes me think of a day, quite recently, when I sat with him in the garden; it was in August and I was showing him photographs of another garden, wondering if he recognised any of the people in the photographs.

I took a few pictures of my father on that day in August. He's not looking great, I thought. Not great.

I was showing him pictures of my aunt Stella's funeral – actually not my real aunt, but my mother's cousin. Like I said, my real aunts, my father's sisters, both died in childhood – so not real aunts, but potential aunts, if such a category exists.

Jesus – Stella. I talked to her the whole time she was in the hospice – a month. Every day, she told me that she just needed a little more treatment, and then she'd go home, and then I could come and see her.

Now, as my father's taxi pulls away, I walk out of the surgery, under a grey sky, and turn left onto the twinkly high street.

Christmas is coming.

Back home, I scroll through the pictures on my phone. A blur of grey, becoming progressively blue. And here's my father, sitting on a garden chair, framed by bushes.

My heart jumps. He looks great.

An Hour

Anyway, Stella. She had cancer. They operated. The operation was declared a success. Then she had a scan. There was a shadow on the scan – a shadow that might or might not have been evidence of cancer. Maybe the cancer had come back. Or maybe they hadn't got all of it the first time around. Or maybe it was nothing.

Stella was advised to have another operation – just to make sure. But she refused. Said she'd rather take her chances. Neither of my parents went to her funeral, citing my father's illness – his inability to go on a long train journey and stay in a hotel. But then, three years earlier, when Stella's husband had died, neither of my parents went to *his* funeral, citing my father's illness – too unwell for the train, the unfamiliar bed. And my mother couldn't go on her own, she said, because she 'had to look after him'. So his illness – his lack of wellness, his invalidity – has been with him for a long time. Three years ago, it was beginning to be part of his identity. One day, I realised, it will *be* his identity, just as it was his identity as a child with rheumatic fever, and then later, as an adult with acute stomach ulcers.

He was healthy between the ages of, roughly speaking, thirty and sixty. He thrived in middle age, full of furtive energy, during the years of disappearance.

I went to the two funerals – Stella's and Stella's husband's – with my brother. I know I haven't said anything about him. There are reasons for this omission. (I am mostly, if not entirely, to blame.) Both times, we travelled together on the train. On the first journey, he got so angry with me – Jesus, so angry I have this memory of him standing up, and his fist clenching; we'd been drinking – and I knew he was going to smash me in the face (partly because he *said* he was going to smash me in the face). But it was more than that – more than the bunched fist and the threat. You can sometimes feel the energy around somebody if you know them well, and there he was, standing above me, and I could feel that energy.

Freeze that image for a moment.

It was my fault. He was four years younger than me. From the age of about ten, for about five years, I persecuted him relentlessly, homing in on the things that triggered his emotions. I was a bad older brother – not least because the problems that tormented me, stemming from my father's constant absences, must also have tormented him. As adults, though, our childhood has been hard to talk about; I want to relive the past, whereas he, I think, wants to put it behind him. I'm always having these imaginary conversations with him.

You can't live in denial, I say.

I don't, he says.

It will end up killing you, I say.

Which makes him want to hit me. When I imagine this, and when it actually happens, I can feel the energy coming off him, feel the fist before it arrives, a not unpleasant sensation, a sort of excitement, an electric current running along my nerves. He's a big guy, too. Well over six feet. An active guy. A guy who drinks, but who also lifts weights, swims, cycles, plays football. He throws himself into tackles; he also launches himself through the air, head first, a missile forcing its way through knees and thighs and boots.

On the way to Stella's husband's funeral, I could see the fist, and I could feel a preview of the fist, feel the current of the fist's intentions running along my nerves, a couple of seconds ahead of time.

We would be at the funeral 'representing the family', because my father was too frail to attend, had after all recently stopped driving, had boosted his intake of spirits, had begun to collapse ('collapse of stout party', my mother said every time it happened). He was beginning the cycle of fainting, followed by the remedy for fainting, mostly rum or brandy. And of course, we would perform the same function at Stella's funeral several years later, when my father was even sicker — even though, at the time, all of this seemed normal, seemed like a gentle decline, like a plane coming in to land. A decline that seems to take for ever.

Stella's decline was much swifter. There was the shadow, followed by the refusal to have an operation. But the shadow was cancer, and it spread, it colonised, and then Stella left home for the last time, and she moved into a hospice. She was in the hospice for thirty-two days, and I called her almost every day.

She told me not to come to visit, because pretty soon she'd get better, and she'd go back home, and *then* I could visit. She talked about getting better, and I talked about my career as a writer, which was, I hoped, on the verge of taking off. One day I interviewed this guy, Adrian Raine, who was an expert on serial killers, and the way I explained it, she said, sounded very promising. For her part, she was painting self-portraits in watercolour.

One day she said she'd changed her mind – I *could* come and see her before she went home.

I caught the train. But when I arrived, she was dead. I'd missed her by an hour.

I showed my father pictures from her funeral, and took some pictures of him. I thought he looked unwell in the pictures, which was true. But now he looks great in those pictures, which is also true.

In Stella's final self-portrait, the face is the face of a person who is close to death. But the painting contains the vitality of a person who is able to capture this face very . . . frankly, I suppose – from *franche*, the Old French word meaning free, as in free to tell the truth.

She was dying – something she did not want to tell me the truth about. No, she wanted to have conversations – we had twenty-eight while she was in the hospice – in which she was not dying, just as I wanted to have conversations in which I was not a struggling writer, but the sort of writer who might interview an expert on serial killers in order to create a series of bestselling crime novels – novels, perhaps, like the ones my father devoured.

In Stella's last picture, the artist is vital, even if the subject is dying. Her picture tells the truth.

A Package

A package arrives at my house. It contains a series of books by the Norwegian writer Karl Ove Knausgaard, and my first reaction, when I look at these books, is dread.

I need to put them on an obscure shelf with the spines facing the wrong way. I need to forget all about them.

I've read the first volume, *A Death in the Family*, which is about the death of Karl Ove's father. At the very start of the book, the author confronts death itself. The name of the whole series is *My Struggle*, translated from the Norwegian *Min Kamp*, with its echoes of *Mein Kampf*, the world's most infamous book.

Death and evil. Reading it now might have a terrible effect. It could damage me – tip me over the line into whatever. A concept flies into my brain, for the umpteenth time, which is: we are the only creature that spends most of its life knowing we must die, and if all the other creatures could vote, and they were asked to name the most evil creature on the planet, they would all, without question, vote for us. Bacteria would vote for us. Lions would vote for us. These other creatures might be predatory, savage, vicious and careless. But we are evil. *Big* difference. We know death. We are intimate with death. This intimacy makes us evil. That's what I keep thinking.

For the shark, death is food. For us, death is death. This fact has twisted our minds.

Anyway, I've already read the first volume of *My Struggle*, and it's haunting. The author starts by confronting facing up to death – the brute fact of it, but what this brute fact does to us. Not just the nature of it, but the culture of it. Death is natural. But the culture of death is something else. Knausgaard does not run away from this. He shows it to us. He displays the culture of death, and when we read this, a powerful sensation enters the reader's brain.

I need to put the books on my top shelf, turned the wrong way around.

But I don't. Somewhere between the hallway and the bookshelf, something changes, and I find myself sitting on the sofa, turning, for a second time, to the opening chapter of *A Death in the Family*.

And *fuck*. It tears into me. First he explains everything that happens after the moment of death, after the heart stops beating. The blood pools at the lowest point. *Rigor mortis* begins. Armies of bacteria invade the organs: 'They advance on the Haversian canals, the crypts of Lieberkuhn, the islets of Langerhans.' Eventually, they arrive at the heart, and 'there is something strangely desolate about it, like a production plant that workers have been forced to flee in haste'. He imagines an abandoned site – the static yellow diggers and dozers, the deserted cabins.

And yes, I keep thinking, this will happen to him, to my father, it will happen to him, really soon, like really soon, and I am filled with this emotion, part of which is to do with my father, his neglect of me, he didn't want me, he explicitly said this, he *did not want children*, and yet there I was, his first; he *did not want me*, and I have never discussed this with him; and then when I was born, he did not—

Oh, what's the use? It's too late now, I think – too late to discuss it with him, or else to do something, to make him notice me, or maybe have a proper talk, a proper chat, to take up where we left off in '79, when he drove me back to the airport, and in the car I actually felt I could say anything to him, like we were friends, and it irks me that I don't hate him, or in any case feel flat and neutral, but I don't, I feel a strange tenderness towards him, my dear old dad I might say, that phrase filling the tear ducts, priming the pump, but I still can't, or won't, cry; the only things that make me cry are strange things, for instance when somebody is being really clever, like the performance of Jesse Eisenberg in *The Social Network*.

In any case, very soon his heart will stop, his breathing will stop, his blood will pool, his limbs will stiffen, and armies of tiny creatures will begin to eat him from the inside, and I don't want this to happen, but it will, and very soon; I don't want it to happen for selfish reasons, I'm sure.

I have failed with him. I want more time. So it's not exactly *him* I will be mourning, but an aspect of *me*.

When a person dies, says Knausgaard, he 'belongs to death'. And this makes him the same as lots of things, things that also belong to death – 'lamps, suitcases, carpets, door handles, windows'. These man-made objects are rendered from formerly living things. But when a person crosses the line and becomes a formerly living thing, an object, we cannot bear it if people see this object. If the body is in hospital, we pull curtains around the bed; if it happens to be outdoors, we cover it with a coat or a blanket; when it must be moved, we drive it in a windowless truck, towards a guarded underground room.

Which means, says Knausgaard, that there are two types of death.

My fingers are gripping the book. It's a dark afternoon. The branches of the trees in my small garden, leafless, are tapping against each other in the dark.

Two types of death. Looking out at the blackness beyond my window, I experience a powerful urge to meet this guy, to talk to him.

I'll call him.

Ersatz Coffee

My father is taken to the hospital for tests. An ambulance picks him up in the morning; supposedly an ambulance will deliver him back later in the day.

I walk the two miles to my parents' house to have a cup of tea with my mother. She is anxious and jittery. For a while we talk about my father's cut, his blood tests, the different pills he takes every day. We also talk about Christmas, but I change the subject quickly, before anything bad happens.

We talk about my son, who stays with me every weekend. She thinks I don't bring him to see her and my father often enough. She might be right. I don't argue.

We have long-running disputes, my mother and I; today, neither of us wants to do battle. So we talk about my father. I have an urge to go over old memories, to see if I can trigger new ones. I ask about his trip to Berlin in 1966, and his trip to Buenos Aires in 1970. Both times, he was accompanied by my mother. We have talked about these trips before. This – the mystery of my father – is, temporarily, safe territory for us. We wouldn't be able to have this conversation in front of him; he would seethe with discomfort. And any sort of discomfort on the part of my father, any tiny thing, absolutely horrifies my mother.

So: Berlin, 1966. They flew into West Berlin, as it says on their passports: Flughafen Tempelhof. (On subsequent trips, my father would fly into Flughafen Schönefeld, on the eastern, Communist side of the border.) But in 1966, they stayed in an expensive hotel, right in the centre of West Berlin. My father had meetings during the day; he and my mother were entertained in the evenings. None of this, she is sure, was sponsored by the UN, or by UNESCO. So probably the German government.

One evening they were taken to see a performance of Mahler at the Berliner Philharmonie.

At this, as in the past, my mother becomes agitated. 'I couldn't believe it! They did the *Kindertotenlieder*! We were sitting with all these Nazis, a lot of them would have been Nazis, and they had the—'

'Yes, yes.'

I'm nodding my head. I'm thinking: *Kinder*, children. *Toten*, death. *Lieder*, songs. All one word. Childrendeathsongs.

(At this point, I should mention the fact that my mother is a *fervent* anti-Nazi – she's right up there. I have identified three reasons.

One: she was born in 1932, which means she was aged between seven and thirteen during the war. So she took the war broadcasts at face value: there was something cruel and conniving embedded in the German culture.

Two: her best friend at school was a Jewish girl from Prague whose family put her on one of the last trains before the Nazis closed in; the family was murdered in the camps. My mother will always signal her emphasis on the word *murdered*, rather than merely *killed*. And think about this for a moment. As the months and years went on, and my mother's friend, at the age of ten, and then eleven, and then twelve, didn't hear from her family, she must have been in a very specific, personal hell, every day bringing with it fresh torment, laced with denial and the poison of hope.

And three: my mother's favourite cousin, George Lee, a navigator in Bomber Command, was shot down over France, and declared 'missing in action'; his death was not made official for years. (Many years later, she went to France with George's brother and searched, successfully, for George's grave. When he died, he was twenty-one, and she was ten; when she found the grave, he was twenty-one, and she was fifty-six.))

'—the *gall*. To sit there in their furs, the women were wearing furs . . . and then this music about dead children! I kept looking at them, all those Nazis, because come *on*, a lot of them would have been Nazis, and I was thinking, I wonder how many children *you* killed . . .'

Kindertotenlieder, I'm thinking. Kindertransport, I'm thinking. (My mother's friend, incidentally, married this very brilliant guy, who had also escaped from the

Nazis, and who invented an essential component used by NASA in their Apollo rockets.)

One day, says my mother, she and my father crossed over into East Berlin. I've heard this part of the story several times, just like I've heard the part about the Nazis in the Berliner Philharmonie several times. My parents went through Checkpoint Charlie. Their passports were taken away. They waited in a room for about an hour. The room was drab. There were guards. Their passports were given back. They were picked up in a car and driven to a big house on the edge of the city. In the house, my mother was told to wait in a downstairs room. Meanwhile, my father went upstairs to meet somebody. My mother was given a cup of what she calls 'ersatz coffee'. She sat alone in the room for more than an hour. In terms of decor, the room was not quite a sitting room, but not quite a waiting room. Then my father came downstairs. The car was waiting outside; a couple of hours later, they were back in their hotel.

I often wondered, and still wonder, about this story. It's half a century old. Has it changed over time? Once or twice I asked my father about it. He dismissed it as something absolutely normal – which it might have been to him, in the light of thirty-odd years of such trips. He was visiting psychologists in Berlin; this one lived in East Berlin, hence the hassle at the border. Yes, he remembered the Mahler concert. Yes, he remembered my mother's anti-Nazi disquiet.

Why did my mother come with him in the car? Probably because she was excited by the whole thing. The chance to bond with my father. She was a young wife. He was a distant husband. Here was something she could share with him.

But. Ersatz coffee. For some reason I don't like that detail.

Anyway, Buenos Aires. August 1970. This trip was sponsored by the United Nations. My father was among a group of psychologists; they were all experts on learning and education. They attended a gala dinner. A politician made a speech. During the daytime, my mother and the other wives were taken on touristy trips – to a beef ranch, and also to watch a fancy jeweller at work. They were given money to spend – in cash. The equivalent of $500, she says. They spent the money on gifts, mostly leather goods (I got a lovely football) and a two-day trip to Rio de Janeiro; this is confirmed in their passports.

'And then those two Americans appeared, one morning, and he went off with them, and didn't come back until the evening.'

I've heard this before, too. She remembers one of the Americans well – Bill M. Even I remember Bill M. I met him twice, or possibly three times, in Swiss and German hotels, in the 1970s. He was a professor of psychology at a Midwestern university. My mother can't remember the other man. In any case, after the arrival of the Americans, my father's plans changed. He didn't fly back from Buenos Aires with my mother, as she was expecting. Instead, he went to America. Then he came back to England two weeks later.

We've been talking for two hours. We have no idea when my father's ambulance will come back. Our anxiety about his condition has spilled into other areas.

'What do you think he was *doing* all that time?' A not unfamiliar question from my mother, with a step more urgency than usual.

'Didn't you ask him?'

'I don't know. Not really.'

'Why not?'

'I don't know. I never found the right—'

I ponder this for a moment.

Then I say: 'Well, he was meeting psychologists. They would be talking about things to do with, you know, what makes people learn things. All that stuff. What makes people believe things.'

'Do you think that's what it was?'

'Something like that.'

As I walk back home, into the darkening afternoon, I think about the Argentinian football. It was perfect. Dark brown. Oblong panels. Soft leather like a woman's jacket. Size four, so a notch smaller than most other balls.

A couple of kids pointed out that it was small. 'That's because it's a size four,' I said, several times.

A man was driving a huge mower, the size of a tractor, the first time I took the ball to the village green. Some kids I knew were kicking around. Then I got into a game with them. We used the Argentinian ball.

One kid lofted the ball into the air. In my memory, everything happens very slowly: the arc of the ball against the sky; the ball dropping perfectly into the space the mower is yet to occupy.

For a second or two I don't know if the ball will bounce off the mower, or if the mower will chew it up.

The mower chews it up.

The Strangest Thing of All

The ambulance came back. My father was fine. Or rather, he was not fine. But he was 'himself'. A man in his later eighties, going downhill, with an infected leg that won't heal, armies of bacteria getting ready for blitzkrieg.

Still, I can't help noticing that we are already settling into a new normal. Like: he is dying. But then, aren't we all? I mean, we spend most of our lives dying, right?

Yeah, right. But he is *actually dying* – and this, too, has come to seem normal, in a rocky sort of way. He has had tests; he is scheduled to have more tests in a few weeks. His regime of medications has been updated. A doctor will visit and explain everything. My mother asks if I can be there, because I'm good at remembering things.

But something *very weird* happens the next day. My father had gone into his bedroom, which is also his study, for an afternoon nap. My mother heard strange noises. Scraping and crashing. My father was on the floor, ransacking an old chest of drawers, having removed one of the drawers. The drawers were full of documents and files, and some of them were now all over the floor. Stranger still, when my mother started talking to him, he seemed to be half asleep, or half dreaming. He woke up gradually, with no memory of what he'd been doing. My mother picked up the files, the A4 cardboard 'document wallets' he favours, and put them away. My father went back to bed.

When I was seventeen, after I got into trouble at boarding school, after my parents came back from Canada to sort things out, my father went to see *his* parents in London. He was fifty. His mother was eighty-three. His father was eighty-five. He only stayed with them for a couple of hours. But he told me the oddest thing. He'd gone upstairs to see his father. He'd found his father on the floor, rummaging through a chest of drawers. Documents everywhere.

'He was half asleep. In a sort of dream state,' my father told me. Three weeks later, the old man collapsed, and went into hospital. A week after that, he was dead.

Thirty-six years later, I ask my mother *which* chest of drawers my father was ransacking.

'Was it the one by the bed? Or the one on the other side of the room?'

'The one on the other side of the room. Why?'

Because, I think to myself, this is all very strange. My father and his father did the same thing, at almost exactly the same age, in almost exactly the same state of panicked somnambulism. Perhaps the strangest thing of all is that they were rifling through the same chest of drawers, thirty-six years apart.

I say: 'I'm just trying to picture it.'

Two men. Father and son. In a waking dream. Documents all over the floor. Half a lifetime apart.

And the same chest of drawers. Stranger yet. But not, I will come to see, the strangest thing of all.

The Deadbeat

I take my son to a place called the Skatehouse, an indoor venue for skateboarders. My son is one of the youngest. He's eight, but he started at six, so he's pretty good. He can 'drop in' fearlessly. Sometimes I watch him from the edge of the concrete bowl, and sometimes not, because even at eight, he likes to give the impression that he's arrived on his own, under his own steam.

So I sit in the lobby and read Karl Ove Knausgaard. He says he thinks his children all arrived with their own personalities fully formed, which I think might be true. My son is confident and optimistic – unlike me, he's not neurotic. I thought I'd make him neurotic. But I didn't. He's also very persistent. When he wants to do something, he works at it until he gets it right – one of the most useful qualities you can have.

I read a passage in which Knausgaard talks about cowardice. His girlfriend got stuck in somebody's bathroom at a party, and nobody could open the door. Somebody would have to kick the door open. Knausgaard knows that person should be him. People gather around the door. But at the last moment, Knausgaard asks another guy to do it, and he does, this other guy, he kicks the door open, and Knausgaard instantly feels an overwhelming sense of shame.

He had been more worried about trying and failing than about not trying. A life lesson. Being afraid of failure begets failure.

I'm wearing a grey hooded top by Nicole Farhi, which looks good, I think, although the sleeves may not hang right, I can't make up my mind. I'm also wearing a navy blue T-shirt with a white logo, and my hair is pretty good. I'm meeting my son's mother outside the Skatehouse afterwards, to hand him over. I think she thinks I'm a deadbeat because my career is not exactly taking off. For instance, I'm trying to write a book, but it's taking too long. I think she smells failure on me, which might be why we're estranged.

My son appears in the lobby. Smiling and happy. We pick up our things. His mother is outside. She looks beautiful. She doesn't look me in the eye. I wonder if she is looking at the visible part of the logo on my T-shirt. I wonder if my sleeves are hanging right – I mean, correctly.

I say: 'How are you?'

'I'm fine, thank you.'

'I've got an idea for a new book.'

She nods her head. At least, I think she does. I hand over the backpack and the skateboard.

'Well, see you soon,' I say.

The German Catch

In 1971, when I was ten, we moved to Germany. As always when we were about to move, my mother sold me the idea like a smiling travel agent. We had a great place to live, it was near the Swiss border, there would be mountains – the Alps! The city was on a lake, we were close to Austria as well as Switzerland, we wouldn't be there for long, everything would go back to normal pretty soon.

At this point, I'd like to apologise to my mother; representing my father's life choices must have been a difficult task. Those moments, when my mother explained what was going to happen, and I listened, sulkily, trying to spot the flaw in her presentation, must have been horrible.

Those precise moments. Thinking about them creates stormy weather in my brain. And fertile territory, over the years, for therapy sessions.

Basically, it was *my father* who was dicking us around. But it was *my mother* I was angry with. You're furious with the platoon sergeant who instructs you about the next day's dangerous patrol, when you should really be angry with the general.

Therapist: 'Interesting. Tell me more.'

Me: 'So when I was eight, my mother says we'll be going to Canada, but don't worry, it's only for a year, maybe less than a year, and then we'll come back.'

Therapist: 'OK . . .'

'And then a few days later, I'd spotted the flaw. I say to her, so that means I won't be going into the same class as Richard and Chris in September. And my mother, she looks anxious, and she says no, I suppose not. So, I say, next year, when we get back, will I go into the same class as Richard and Chris *then*? Or will I go into the one *I would have gone into*?'

Therapist: 'And what did she say?'

Me: 'She didn't know what to say, exactly. That I wasn't going back to my old school at all. That, in fact, she didn't know where I'd be going to school – which school, in which town, any of it. Or when I would see Richard and Michael and Chris again. In fact, I wouldn't see them for years – not until graduate school, when I was in my twenties.'

Therapist: 'And how did that make you feel?'

Me: 'Angry. Furious. She'd said we were *coming back*. But to me, we were not coming back at all. We were going somewhere, and then going somewhere *else*. I had believed I was going to come back to my world. Now I could see I was going to lose my world.'

The Canadian catch was that, after we went to Canada, we weren't coming back. We were going somewhere else. That was the Canadian catch.

The German catch was that, after we all went to Germany to be with my father, one of us would have to go back to England, in order to go to boarding school. And that person, of course, would be me.

But I didn't feel angry with my father. I felt various things. Curiosity about him. A need to be noticed. A sort of emptiness.

The Knock at the Door

March 1971. My father lives in a big modern apartment in a quiet part of Konstanz, close to the university campus. And also close to the Swiss border, the Rhine bridge, the big lake.

It's nice, even though I feel haunted by the fact that, in four and a half weeks, I will be taken to the airport at Zurich, flown to England, taken to boarding school. I will live in a dormitory. Which is not nice at all.

I cannot imagine how this sequence will play out. Or how it will feel.

Anyway, we explore the apartment. My brother, who is six, takes me into the bathroom.

'What's that?'

He points to the ledge in the toilet bowl. A porcelain ledge. Usually, when you evacuate your bowels, everything just falls down into the water, and then you flush it away. Here, it lands on the ledge, so that you can inspect it.

I say: 'If you do a poo, and it touches the ledge, it can go back inside you.'

He looks up at me.

'If that happens . . . you might die.'

I look into his little face. 'Just be careful, OK.'

'OK.'

I am *not a nice person*.

On weekdays, my father leaves the apartment early and returns late. He is working on a project with a very clever man called Karl-Heinz, who we sometimes see at the weekends. (Karl-Heinz is developing an intricate psychological model of 'didactic action' – how ideas can be transferred from one person's mind to another's.) He has a wife called Ursula, and two boys, Stefan and Tillmann, aged seven and nine.

We go on day trips. We go across the lake. There are three islands in the lake. We visit all of them. We visit Austria. We drive around Switzerland. We go up a mountain in a cable car. I hate cable cars. I can't even stand watching people getting into cable cars on TV. I have to leave the room. When you're in a cable car, there is all this space above and below you, and you are trapped in a box.

After about two weeks, my brother starts making strange noises. Then he falls to the ground and can't get up. My mother calls an ambulance.

He's OK. The doctors give him an enema. There is a physical enema, in which the contents of his bowels are flushed out, and also a mental one, in which the doctors flush out the reason for his constipation.

I'm in disgrace.

One day we visit a medieval church, and something terrible happens to my mind. The church, which is cold and bleak and smells of ancient stone, is decorated with elaborate images of death – a *Totentanz,* or *danse macabre*, a procession of skeletons designed to remind the churchgoer of his or her mortality. My mind is jolted by a single, stark fact. The skeletons depict a central truth.

Looking back at this moment, which would lead to a night of inconsolable crying, followed by several nights of acute misery, followed by a general feeling of doom that lasted for years, I ask myself a couple of questions.

The first question is: was the central truth depicted in the *Totentanz* really the focus of my misery?

Well, maybe.

My aunt Stella was coming to visit us. She would stay a week. Then she would take me away.

Now, when I think of the *Totentanz*, I think of the people who painted it, maybe 500 years ago, and what happened after they painted all those skeletons: their lives, and the lives of generations of their descendants, just disappeared, one after the other, all these lives scythed into eternity, and I think of how, when you die, you enter this eternity, time having absolutely no meaning for the dead; when I die, I will enter a timeless realm, and this thought, of time having no meaning, is primally frightening.

Did any of this primal fear enter my mind when I looked at the dancing skeletons, ten days before my eleventh birthday?

That's the second question.

In any case, I stopped crying, and one day, in the middle of the afternoon, there was a knock at the door.

A Veil Had Lifted

When I was in my early forties, the age my father was when he moved to the apartment in Konstanz, I began to be very angry about my childhood. A veil had lifted; feelings that had been muffled – partly by alcohol – took on new, sharper, dimensions.

That was when I started to be obnoxious towards my mother – I'd make dark comments over lunch when I came to visit, or recommend books about people who'd had bad childhoods. But I was never obnoxious towards my father. He was vulnerable, said my mother. He had told her, deep in the past, that he was bullied at school, and also that the subject was never to be mentioned again. Anything negative, such as a discussion about boarding school, might push him over the edge.

He was a master of denial. He put things out of his mind. Like they never happened. It wasn't just the bullying. It was everything about his childhood. He was always running away from anything that reminded him of his childhood.

Anyway, my mother. When, much later, on Sunday afternoon walks, I said negative things about dormitories, or about nasty schoolmasters, she would say something like: 'Well, there was always the holidays.' Or: 'It was only a few weeks at a time.' And I can't blame her for saying those things. She had a stable childhood, with both parents in the house every night, the same set of friends for years, a live-in grandmother, a long-term boyfriend and a dog. She was one of those people who was liked in equal measure by teachers and classmates. If, for some reason, she'd had to go away for a few weeks, she might well have been fine.

For years I tried, and failed, to explain why I wasn't. I drew a blank until my early forties. Having quit drugs (a nasty cocaine habit), I was trying to quit alcohol. I went to see a therapist twice a week; she was an ideal mixture of intellect and empathy. Gradually, she drew things out of me; I, too, had been a master of denial. (Even when I was trying to be as open as possible!)

And here it was: if you go to boarding school, and you don't want to go to boarding school (and some people do, some people like it, I've always known *that*), but if you don't want to, if you don't like the idea, your life changes for the worse. Well, duh. But the change is not just located in the school environment. *School* is not the only problem. *Home* becomes a problem, too.

Home stops being a longed-for escape ('only a few weeks'). Home is now the place that sent you away. Logically, you can tell yourself that it's not your parents' fault, that this had to happen, that there was no alternative and so on. And logically, yes, this might all make sense. But there's an emotional level, too. You might not be able to access this emotional level; your brain will almost certainly try to hide it from you. But it will always be there. Home is now different. Boarding school, with its constant throb of sex and violence, is a frightening and degenerate world. But you know that; it is what it is. But home – home is no longer an Eden. Home pretends to be an Eden, but it is full of snakes.

It is not what it is.

But I want to apologise to my mother. I don't blame her. Not really. Not much. It's my father I should blame. He wasn't thinking about me. He was thinking about Karl-Heinz, about didactic action, about the most efficient way to convey ideas from one person's mind to another's.

But do I blame him? Not really. Not much.

My mother asked me, after the paedophile scandal at my school, why I hadn't thought to say anything, to mention my misgivings. One of the masters was a cast-iron paedophile; he'd been looking in our shorts and groping us for years. Eventually he turned Humbert (or rather a gay Humbert): he abducted a boy and took him on a cross-country drive. He was arrested. He went to jail.

But were there others who weren't arrested? Possibly. One man awarded himself the task of supervising us in the shower. He timed us; to get dressed in the three allotted minutes, you had to forget about modesty. You had a choice: modesty cost you three blows on the palm of your hand with the sharp edge of a ruler. I chose modesty, every time, and came away with painful manual beatings. Others sat damply through the next lesson.

But, see, I didn't know what paedophiles were. I didn't even know the *word*. So if I had fears (and I did) about going to boarding school, I wouldn't have known how to explain those fears.

I was in the apartment on the Jacob-Burckhardt Strasse in Konstanz. I was ten. There was a knock on the door. It was Stella.

Running Out of Options

Forty-three years and eight months later, I'm standing in my parents' garden extension. My father sits in his favourite chair, a brown corduroy La-Z-Boy. He wears his now familiar glazed expression, to which he has added a benign half-smile. My mother is in the kitchen. Karl-Heinz has been dead for two years; his son, Stefan, died of a brain tumour two decades ago; Stella's final self-portrait is stacked between framed pictures that have never made it onto the wall. I no longer drink. On one level, I think, my brother hates me. In a few days' time, it will be Christmas.

There is a knock on the door. It's the doctor.

He is young, blond, in his late twenties. His face is unreadable. We all sit down. My mother brings tea.

The doctor explains my father's symptoms and medications. He has a cut that won't heal. The cut is infected. He needs to get rid of the infection. He needs his blood to clot. But: he has a heart problem. He needs his blood not to clot. So he takes warfarin, to stop his blood from clotting. But: taking warfarin means he can't take the antibiotics he needs to get rid of the infection. It's also stopping his cut from healing. So: he should stop taking warfarin, and start taking antibiotics. On the balance of probability, that's the best thing to do. Yes, it's rolling the dice. But we're running out of options.

That's the gist of what the doctor says. When he leaves, I show him to the door.

In the kitchen, I say: 'That's what I said!'

My mother: 'What did you say?'

'That he should stop taking the warfarin!'

She looks at me quizzically. Outside, the doctor starts his car, executes a three-point turn and drives away. My father is still sitting in the armchair, still wearing his glazed expression, still almost, but not quite, smiling. He has been silent throughout the doctor's visit. He has twenty-four days to live.

Something Really Nasty

Forty-three years earlier, exactly half of my father's lifespan, Stella walks into the apartment on the Jacob-Burckhardt Strasse. She will spend the next week walking by the lake, seeing the mountains, and visiting an exhibition of paintings by Paul Klee. Then she will accompany me on the train to Zurich, and on a plane to England. She will drop me off at school and go home. Not long after this, while teaching an evening class, she will meet a man. When he dies, four decades later, my father will be too unwell to attend his funeral. I will go to the funeral with my brother. On the train my brother will stand up, the fingers of his right hand clenching into a fist. I will feel the energy coming off him, the electricity of malice. To stop him smashing me in the face, I will need to do something. Something really nasty.

Three Scenes from Prep School

I'm at a prep school, which stands for preparatory school, a school that is trying to *prepare* me for something, in this case a public school, which actually means a private school, where I will be educated alongside children whose parents, for whatever reason, have a significant amount of spare money.

Oh, I know that thing: 'We scrimped and saved! The local schools were just so awful!' I know that thing.

I'm standing in a Victorian gymnasium, with a parquet floor and wooden climbing bars up the side of the wall. It's chilly. I'm in a line of boys wearing gym clothes. The master who takes the gym class is addressing the line of boys. Under no circumstances, he tells us, are we to wear underpants under our gym shorts. But because some boys might want to break these rules, he has no choice but to conduct a random inspection.

We stand still in a line while he prowls the area in front of us. He is tall, and sort of sloppy-looking, with frizzy dark hair and long sideburns. He moves towards us and walks along the line and back again. The line is still. The gym is silent apart from the master's footsteps and his ragged breathing when he comes close.

He hates me, I think, because when he tried to grope my shoulders and chest, when I was sitting at a desk for evening prep (short for preparation, from the Latin *prae*, before, and *parare*, to make something ready), I hit him.

Now he makes his first choice: a boy to the right of me, maybe four boys along the line. He bends forward, pulls on the elasticated waist of the boy's shorts, lowers his head towards the boy's midriff, and peers into the gap. Seeing what he wants to see, he raises himself to his full height, around six feet, and says the word 'good' followed by the boy's surname.

He is in his thirties. A pervert. (From the Latin *pervertere*: to turn the wrong way – *per*, away, and *vertere*, to turn.)

He passes me and chooses the boy to my left, repeating the procedure. I can hear the jumps of air in his trachea as his head goes down. Then: the peering; the snap of the elastic; the positive approbation; the boy's surname.

A pervert. He has *turned the wrong way*. He has strayed from the righteous path. This much is obvious. He is sliding towards a point of no return, when control and decorum will evade him. His mind is sorting and cataloguing boys and their characteristics, preparing for the moment when his disgrace will be complete, the moment of pouncing, of snatching, of abducting. This much is not obvious.

Another scene. I'm in a dormitory, in bed, propped up by an elbow. One boy is talking; others are listening. The boy is Asian. He says he's been told, by his uncle, that women have 'seven gateways' between their legs. He takes us through each of the gateways, starting from the outside. First, a curtain of fine hair. Next, an outer set of lips. Proceeding inwards, a second set of lips, much more delicate than the first. After this, an outer mouth, and then an inner mouth, followed by a funnel, which squeezes open and closed. Finally, the innermost entrance of all – the entrance to the womb.

After a while, we drift off to sleep. The next day, a boy says to me: 'I didn't think there were *seven*. I would have said five.'

A third scene. I'm in the dining hall, sitting at my table. It's lunchtime. There are eight people at my table. The headmaster – the HM – is sitting at his own, raised table at the end of the room. To the side of his plate is a little gong. Next to the gong is a little mallet.

The rule is that, when the HM hits the gong with the mallet, everybody must stop speaking. If you speak after the gong has rung, the HM will ask you to leave the dining hall immediately and wait outside the room he calls his 'study'. Then, after the meal is over, he will come and find you and beat you.

The meal is underway. The first course has been served. I'm telling a joke. I'm one word away from the end of the joke. That one word is the punchline.

The HM is fairly new. He has been at the school for a couple of terms. He is a portly man of authority, a stickler for rules; I have heard him described as a 'muscular Christian'. He favours discipline and prayer. In rugby, he played in the scrum. On the field, he has taught us the manly codes of rucks and mauls.

The next bit happens very fast. The HM picks up the mallet and bangs the gong. I don't see him picking up the mallet. But I hear the gong. The hall goes silent. I say the word. Seven people let out a sharp snap of laughter.

. The HM tells me to leave the hall immediately and wait outside his study. I have had three or four bites of my lunch. Flushed, holding back tears, I walk between two rows of chair backs, across the hall, and out of the door.

Outside the dining hall, the school is silent. I could go anywhere for half an hour, but I stand by the HM's door. When he finally comes, full of meat and custard pudding, he tells me to bend over an armchair and whacks me three times on the bottom with a tennis shoe. The pain is a relief, an emotional release, but I will not let him see me cry.

Something I Have Never Done

When my parents get back from Germany, we spend part of the summer holiday in Cambridge, with my father's old friend Dr Khan, and also his wife and toddler son.

Dr Khan, whose marriage was arranged, is a moral philosopher. He's probably the best guy I ever met in my life. He will fall in love with my mother; I will get to know him well; we will become confidants; we will have many discussions about good and evil; about right and wrong; he will move to Australia; he will die of cancer. But all this is in the future. In the summer of 1971, he is a visiting fellow in the philosophy department. He comes from a diamond-trading background in Mumbai.

We are in a complex of residential buildings surrounded by gardens. Every day I explore the gardens. They go on and on; you could walk for miles by going from garden to garden. During the day, we walk around the town and along the river. In the evening, we sit around a big table.

My father is sulky. He won't talk to me. I keep trying. One afternoon I do something I have never done. I ask him what the matter is. He says he can't tell me. I ask him why. He stares at me. He is silent for what seems a long time. Shortly after this, he will move to Holland. The rest of us will not go with him.

Finally – and I can remember the precise tone of voice, the harshness and pain in the tone of voice – he says: 'Because you'll blab.'

Back to His Words

I'm sitting in my parents' kitchen extension, having a rare conversation with my father, who has three weeks left to live. He has, I'm pretty sure, lost weight, but his face is still slightly chubby; at some angles, he looks fine. There is a stillness about him. But sometimes his eyes glitter and he seems to come alive. Also, he appears to have stopped drinking. The last drink I saw him take, two or three weeks ago, was a Campari, a generous measure with a few drops of water. Now he drinks black tea.

The conversation is mundane. I don't want it to be mundane. I feel like a striker in the penalty box, waiting for the ball to come my way. But it never does.

My mother has gone shopping. When she comes back, my father gets up and makes his way, slowly, up to his study.

She asks how he is feeling.

He extends his hand, palm down, and tilts it from side to side.

Picking his way across the hall, he says: 'Onwards and upwards.' He tackles the stairs as if they are made of ice, as if he is wearing crampons.

After a while, my mother says: 'Back to his words.'

Barbarians

They met when they were students, at what was then King's College, Durham, more recently the University of Newcastle. She was eighteen; he was twenty-three. War service had set him back a few years. He'd been in the Navy at the end of the war, was on a ship, had sailed towards the combat zone. But then the war ended. As a child, I saw this as very bad luck – to come so close, and then not to fire a single shot, or even be on the ship while the shots were *being* fired. All it would have taken, I kept thinking, was a few more days.

When my parents met, my mother was engaged to a guy called Colin. They'd been an item since the age of ten. Colin was the sort of guy who would like, and be liked by, the sort of girl – in other words my mother – who rode horses and played netball. My father had never been near a horse. But she said she was attracted to his mind. He was a thinker. He would listen to Bach, and try to understand the relationship between the music and the brain of the person listening to the music. How could a sequence of noises so reliably convey such a precise suite of emotions?

My mother had never met anybody who thought like this. Colin had liked Frank Sinatra, card games and dancing. He played snooker and bridge. He kept in touch with my mother for the rest of his life. I met him when I was a teenager. By then, he ran a reinsurance company in Cape Town. He was rich. But the advent of my father had destroyed him emotionally. Years later, when he was in his sixties, he called my mother and told her to think of him the next day, because he was about to have heart surgery. He said, wrongly, that it would be a straightforward operation.

Anyway, my father's mind. He was a very precise thinker. He would take a subject and draw a box around it. Then he would try to understand everything inside the box. He did his first degree in philosophy, and then moved on to psychology. He wanted to understand how the mind worked. Was the mind a machine?

Possibly.

My father would sit in a chair, or at a desk, just thinking. Not even taking notes. But just thinking. He once told me a story about a famous philosopher – I can't remember who, although the name lurks somewhere, under the surface. Anyway, this philosopher would spend about eight hours every day sitting in an armchair, and his landlady, this must have been when the guy was a student, his landlady said, 'Why don't you *do* something?' and I'm not telling this right, it's my father's story, but the guy said something like, 'Madam, haven't you ever heard of thinking?'

Or maybe: 'I *am* doing something. I'm thinking.'

Whatever. The point is that for my father, thinking was a form of action.

When my mother introduced my father to her family, he sat in a chair and said nothing. My grandfather walked over to him.

He said: 'Why don't you let the rest of us get a word in?'

Later, when my mother asked my father what he thought of her family, he was silent for a moment.

Then he said: 'They are barbarians.'

Pillar-Boxes

One way to get a glimpse inside my father's mind is to read the philosophical paper 'When to Use the Paradigm-Case Argument', which he co-wrote with a philosopher called H. S. Eveling shortly after my parents were married. The paper was published in *Analysis*, the philosophical journal based in Oxford.

When I was a philosophy student, people often talked about papers published in *Analysis*; the fact that my father had a paper in *Analysis* made me – what? I was going to say 'proud'. But that's not exactly right. Something, anyway. A thing I can't describe with perfect precision. But, anyway, a thing.

In 'When to Use the Paradigm-Case Argument', my father and Mr E. stage a thought experiment.

'Consider the case of the philosopher,' they write, 'who, for some reason or other, decided that GPO pillar-boxes are not red but claims to understand what everyone else means when they use the adjective "red" and can use the term correctly in his turn, being aware that everyone who uses the language has said of GPO pillar-boxes, that they are red.'

Reading this now, sitting on my sofa, it baffles me, although I have a faint memory of a time when I could make sense of it.

So, OK. Let's say I'm a philosopher. I have *decided* that pillar-boxes are not red. (From the Latin *de*, meaning off, and *caedere*, to cut. So when you decide, you make a decision – in other words, you cut off, or get rid of, all the avenues you're *not* going to take.)

So: I'm a philosopher. I have made my decision – my *choice*. To me, pillar-boxes are not red. But I claim to know what everybody else means when they use the word 'red'.

My father and Mr E. then say: 'What the paradigm-case argument maintains is *not* that it is inconsistent to deny the redness of pillar-boxes, but that it is inconsistent to deny this whilst admitting that the vast majority of persons who understand the language would say that they are red, and that what they mean by "red" is what the person who denies they are red means by it.'

In other words (I think), if you deny that pillar-boxes are red, you are not saying that red things are not red. You're merely saying that 'things that other people think are red' are not necessarily red.

Scratch that. Maybe not. I need to think about this pillar-box thing more clearly. Then I can bring it up in conversation with my father the next time I see him.

My mother says she could hear my father and Mr E. in my father's study, back in the 1950s, talking about pillar-boxes into the small hours. Sometimes she would knock on the door and offer the two men a cup of tea.

The pillar-boxes and the study. The men in the study. The girl who rode horses and played netball. A glimpse inside my father's mind. A glimpse inside my father's marriage.

Away from the Flock

Whenever my father did something questionable, or unexpected, or egregious (from the Latin *e*, away, and *grex*, the flock), my mother would tell me that it was because of his bad childhood. He suddenly moved to Canada: it was because of his bad childhood. Ditto Germany: bad childhood. Ditto Holland. Ditto Canada again. And why did he disappear to all those other places? Because he was driven by something, some inner force, driven to do something, to achieve something – something in Nigeria, in Bulgaria, in Egypt, in Kenya, in the Soviet Union, in Czechoslovakia, in the Deutsche Demokratische Republik; he was driven to do something, to achieve something, on behalf of the United Nations, and this drive was a compensatory force, an attempt to cancel the bad things that happened to him in his early years – the tragedy, the fallout from the tragedy, the dead sisters, the silence of the dead sisters, the silence of his mother, the silence of his father, the silence and the secrecy, an entire childhood based on secrecy, a childhood in which one did not talk about things, a moribund world compounded by illness, hospitals, injections, bedside vigils, gradual recovery, complicating glandular problems, fevers, rashes, embarrassing metabolic disorders, bullying, long periods spent in the bedroom, the bedroom the only safe place, because outside the bedroom door was the zone of silence, his mother's chastising silence and his father's despairing silence, so no wonder, you might say, no wonder he rarely saw his parents after he left home, no wonder he did not want children of his own, did not come to see me when I was born, could not talk to me when I was growing up about certain things, many things, most things.

When my father did something questionable, or unexpected, or egregious, it was always about his childhood.

Corpus Christi

I often ask myself: does all this, the sum of him, in some way explain the sum of me? Does it help to explain *my* perpetual distance from the flock? Does it explain the fact that I've pretty much never had a normal job, that I've never quite settled down, that I've been engaged four times but never married, that I've often been obsessed with travel, with getting away from the place I'm in, that I've spent years taking drugs, another form of escape, and drinking, yet another; that I lost a decade of my life to drink and drugs; that I'm only just, at the age of fifty-three, growing up, becoming an adult?

And why am I estranged from the mother of my son?

Something bad happened in my early thirties. I don't know what it was. But I do know what it was. But I don't. But I do. But I don't.

These whining thoughts are haranguing me as I walk the Christmas streets, two weeks before my father's death. On one level I know he will die very soon. But on another level I've slipped into a temporary holding pattern of mild denial. The knowledge that my father does not have long, not long at all – that this, for instance, will definitely be his last Christmas – exists as a feeling below the surface. Sometimes it protrudes like a shark's fin. This state of knowing but not knowing acts on the brain like a mild depressant; I feel as if I am crying, but without the physical symptoms of crying.

In any case, I don't like Christmas. Oddly, I would like it much more if it was a hardcore religious ritual, if it was about the birth of the baby who would be crucified, the joy of his birth mixed with the horror of his death.

I'm not religious myself, even though I spent years in educational establishments dedicated to this guy, one institution in particular being named after his actual body – meaning, I suppose, his dead body.

Now I'm in a shopping centre, with pop music – Christmas songs – emanating from hidden speakers. Like most pop music, the songs hit a tone of melancholy and nostalgia. Pop music, if you want to know the truth, is about the loss of love – or, at the very least, the fear of the loss of love. That's how it works.

I'm looking into a shop window, listening to 'I Wish It Could Be Christmas Everyday', by Wizzard. It strikes me, not for the first time, that this sounds like a song about addiction: 'I wish it could be Christmas every day'; what is that? Wanting something to lift the spirits, you find yourself wanting the same thing all the time, over and over, until you need it just to feel normal, an ordinary day not being good enough any more, no, you need it to be Christmas Day, over and over, with the gifts and the cards and the love and the twinkling lights; it's like the grim reality inhabited by the habitual cocaine user. And what are the first lines of the song? It's about a snowman bringing the snow, which is exactly the wrong way round; the snowman doesn't *bring* the snow, he *is* the snow; the only sort of snowman who *brings* the snow is the man who brings the 'snow', which is what people used to call cocaine in the 1970s, when the song was written. I'm not saying any of this is true. I'm saying: wouldn't it be funny if it *was* true – because, if so, the song, instead of being just another shallow ditty, would actually be an incredibly astute comment on the nature of our modern Christmas, and by extension, the modern world itself, an orgy of increasing appetite and diminishing returns.

I can see the reflection of my face, alternately paler and darker in the flickering seasonal lights, as the song builds towards its climax, in which the singer imagines a world in which we might persuade Santa to stay, to never go away, because if this were to happen, if Santa never actually went away, and we found ourselves frozen in time, at the exact moment of receiving a gift . . . then what?

The Gift

I need to get my father a gift. The last gift I will ever give him. And I know what I want to get him, too – a copy of *Through the Language Glass* by Guy Deutscher. It's exactly the sort of thing my father likes, and has liked all his life – the top end of popular science. He read dozens of these books – and, for obvious reasons, I read them too.

The Selfish Gene by Richard Dawkins; *The Territorial Imperative* by Robert Ardrey; *Silent Spring* by Rachel Carson; *Entropy* by Jeremy Rifkin and Ted Howard; *The Structure of Scientific Revolutions* by Thomas Kuhn; *Guns, Germs and Steel* by Jared Diamond; *Ice, the Ultimate Human Catastrophe* by Fred Hoyle; *The Naked Ape* by Desmond Morris; *The Assault on Truth* and *Final Analysis*, Jeffrey Masson's books on Freud.

Which reminds me of something; it's at the edge of my memory.

In any case, I imagined having conversations with my father, in which we would discuss the subject matter of these books, perhaps accompanied by a couple of glasses of whisky or brandy – although, of course, this last bit would now be impossible, or at least ill advised, for both of us. These discussions almost happened a few times; the subjects were touched on, and quickly dropped, just as we sometimes had brief conversations about the police procedurals and other crime thrillers he loved. I loved these books too, and even interviewed his favourite writers – Elmore Leonard, Ed McBain, Lawrence Block, Harlan Coben – who had become some of my favourite writers in the meantime.

There's a great conversation we could have, I kept thinking. I like to think we still could have this conversation, although time is running out. I must seize the day.

'The thing about Kuhn,' I could begin, with a sly confidence.

Or: 'Elmore Leonard gave me a really good tip for writing a scene.'

Or: 'Lawrence Block told me how to manage my time if I wanted to write a book.'

Or: 'What Rifkin says about the Second Law of Thermodynamics . . .'

Or: 'Feynman puts it brilliantly when he says . . .'

Or: 'Just like Sapir and Whorf said . . .'

Actually, the theories of Edward Sapir and Benjamin Lee Whorf, American linguists prominent in the 1950s, were the happiest hunting ground for me: I can picture a conversation I had with my father, an actual conversation, in which I made Sapir's point that, for a Frenchman, the world is not an Englishman's world with different labels.

I was sitting in the kitchen extension of my parents' house, somewhere in the middle of my difficult thirties.

'It's not the same world, but with different labels,' I said. 'It's a different world.'

And then my father turned the conversation towards Charles Sanders Peirce; he said the name should be pronounced the American way, like the first part of the name 'Percy.' He said this with a smile. We were getting along. A word, a smile, a moment. It stuck in my mind. Just like that Freud thing, which I can now remember.

When I was eighteen, I went to see my father in Canada. Having lived there with my mother for a few years, he was now living there alone. He picked me up at the airport. He was driving a Ford. Before we got to his house, he stopped at a roadside steak restaurant. I remember the name: the Ponderosa Steak House. Ponderosa means heavy, or massive. We had these massive steaks. My father said he believed the restaurant used some kind of tenderising agent in the meat. He said that the next day, he'd be going to the college campus, and that he'd arranged for a guy, a priest, to show me around the town. When we'd finished the steaks, he drove to his house, which was in some woods angled above a river. We went into the house. There wasn't much stuff in the house, apart from in the study and the basement. There was a sunken living room, or I suppose lounge, very 1970s, with a huge fireplace, and a brown corduroy reclining chair, a La-Z-Boy. There were two boxed sets of books on the mantelpiece above the fireplace, one at each end. On one of the boxes was a picture of a youngish guy with a beard. The other had a picture of what looked like the same guy when he was old, when the beard had turned grey.

'Freud when he was young,' said my father. 'And when he was old.' Then he said something else, something about sometimes identifying with one version of Freud, and sometimes with the other, which I didn't understand, but which I've often thought about. There we were, talking about Freud, in his strange sunken lounge. I was eighteen. He was in his early fifties, the age I am now. Over the next month, we would become closer than we ever had been before, or ever would be again. The rest was all downhill.

So what are the chances that we, my father and I, might have a proper conversation now, before he dies, having failed to have this conversation for decades? Or rather: I have failed to have this conversation. The truth might be that he has succeeded in avoiding it.

A case in point: the last time I bumped into him on a walk. I was crossing a road. I looked up. There was my father, with nineteen months to live, on the other side of the road. He was walking slowly.

I crossed the road.

'Hey.'

His head swivelled. He looked at me. Not exactly with displeasure. But not exactly with delight. In the decade before that, we had met for lunch precisely twice in a flat I was renting as a study. The first time, he carried a bag. In the bag was a plastic container of sandwiches my mother had made for us. We ate the sandwiches quite quickly, as if we were refugees who had found a box of sandwiches. Then he left. The second time, I tried, with moderate success, to cook steaks. He ate his steak. So it wasn't a total failure. I think there were green vegetables. Then he went.

I never got the feeling that these meetings were opportunities for conversations to flow. They felt more like moments of snatched time. We met. We ate. That was that. The sandwiches: they stuck with me, those sandwiches. Corned beef and tomato on wholemeal bread.

I can still taste them, those sandwiches. Of course I can't.

But the emotion. I can taste the emotion.

Anyway, there he is, standing on the other side of the street. We live two or three miles apart, but this meeting is vanishingly rare. He turns his head.

I finish crossing the street. On the other side I ask him what he's been doing. He says he's been making photocopies.

OK, I say. What next? He says he's going to the bus stop. From where we're standing, we can see the bus stop. I ask him when his bus arrives. He looks at his watch.

'Forty minutes,' he says.

'How about a coffee?' I say. From where we're standing, we can see the nearest cafe. There is another cafe in the station, which is right beside the bus stop. The cafe in the station will be open, but empty.

He refuses.

He wants, he says, to stand at the bus stop for forty minutes. A man of eighty-five, who feels tired a lot of the time, who sometimes collapses in his armchair and must be revived by a shot of brandy, would rather, when faced with the choice of sitting in a cafe and having a conversation with me, or standing at a bus stop for forty minutes on an October afternoon—

I need to stop thinking about this. It doesn't do me any good.

In the bookshop, I locate the Guy Deutscher book. The blurb on the back says: 'It's a question that has baffled, engaged and fascinated in equal measure for over a century: does the language you speak affect the way you think?'

In other words: is something red because it's red – or because people say it's red? The question posed by my father and Mr E., by Edward Sapir, Benjamin Lee Whorf, and Charles Sanders Peirce. Pronounced 'Perce.'

I fantasise about my father's face on Christmas Day. He will look at the book; he will raise his eyebrows; his eyes will move upwards from the book until they meet mine.

The hint of a smile will be visible in his cheeks, and in the corners of his mouth.

Then I will seize the day.

The Dutch Years

The Dutch years, when my father was based in Holland, when I hardly saw him, when he would go all over the world and send postcards, were the best three years of my childhood. I was twelve, thirteen and fourteen. I lived with my mother and brother and went to day school. For a while, I didn't believe my luck. I was still a little anxious. But then I began to be more carefree. For a couple of years, I could breathe easily. I could see a path forward. But that all ended very suddenly, when I went to boarding school for the worst few years of my childhood – the years when I was fifteen, sixteen and seventeen. During these years, I took many blows – psychologically, I mean. Of course, there were physical blows – but I gave as many of those as I took. People worry way too much about physical blows. And of course way too little about psychological ones. After boarding school I took a gap year. When I was eighteen I visited my father in his house in Nova Scotia. Then I went to university for six years.

The life of an extremely privileged person, you might say.

After university, in my twenties, I was pretty happy. I was still pretty happy on my thirtieth birthday. Thirty-one was fine. Thirty-two started out OK. But then something happened.

I crashed.

I lost the next decade. Now, at the age of fifty-three, I'm still catching up.

In my memory, I loved the Dutch years. My father moved to Utrecht, where he lived in a place called the Villa Fatima. A sort of Graham Greene location, I thought. We never went to the Villa Fatima. There was talk, for about a month, of the possibility that we might go to an international school, where everybody spoke English. The idea was quietly shelved. My father rarely sent postcards from the Villa Fatima. But he sent them from lots of other places – Kenya, Japan, Spain, Alaska. Several times he sent pictures of art treasures from the Smithsonian museum in Washington, DC; he kept visiting a guy at the University of Maryland. There were also postcards from Boston – Beacon Hill, I remember, looking just like a generic picture of London. Once, having been in Spain, he got us each a miniature military figure – 'Madelman', a tiny version of Action Man. You could dress and undress Madelman. His flesh was pink, and he had moulded white underpants, with a hint of a bulge – an improvement on Action Man's pink, featureless crotch.

My mother said that my father would come home 'at weekends'. He did come to see us occasionally. But I never got the sense that he was coming home. He was visiting. Mostly, we went to see him, once or twice a year, in Swiss, German and French cities, the locations of conferences and seminars – Heidelberg, Paris, Lausanne and Fribourg, which is north of Montreux in Switzerland, not the same thing as Freiberg in Germany.

Typically, we would arrive at the hotel – not a smart hotel, but better than average. My father wouldn't be there. He'd be somewhere else. We would walk around the town. Old buildings, steep stone steps, cafes with bright awnings. There was always a spot with a terrific view. We would search for this spot, and then look at the view. We went into churches. Sometimes we would have dinner with my father and his colleagues in a restaurant. We might talk to Karl-Heinz, or Bill M. Sometimes we went out to organised events, like one particular Mozart concert in Heidelberg, where the music was played on eighteenth-century instruments, and where a woman appeared out of nowhere and threw her arms around my father. Other times my parents would go out in the evenings and leave us in the hotel. Once I broke into the hotel kitchen and stole a rack of bread rolls which were joined together. Once my little brother wouldn't stop crying because he thought my parents weren't coming back. That might have been the night I stole the bread rolls. We couldn't eat many of them. We threw them at each other. After a week, or maybe ten days, we'd fly back to England. My father would stay on. Then, at some point, my brother and I would each get a postcard from somewhere in the world.

One day, when I was fourteen, I got the worst news of my life. My mother took me aside. She said she had something to tell me. The thing was that my father wanted to move. He would no longer be living in Utrecht, in the Villa Fatima, but in Nova Scotia. He was planning to go over there and look for somewhere to live. We would go over there too, and help him find a house. Which sounded like fun, didn't it? There would be lakes and beaches.

Lakes. And beaches. And of course, there was a flaw.

My Little World

I don't want to drink. I'm sitting at home, and it's dark outside, a midwinter blackout. I'm feeling sad. Is that the word? My father is creeping towards death, the cut on his leg is still infected, the cut won't heal, the infection is establishing itself, it has seen off several waves of antibiotics. Bacteria are massing; my father is surrounded by millions of warriors, with their battle cries.

Of course they don't have battle cries. They just eat into his leg, and make him feel sick. I can imagine it, a brittle sickness, a weariness; I wonder if he thinks it will strike soon, and finish him off, or if he thinks it will just get gradually worse. Or if he tries not to think about it.

I think about it.

But I don't want to drink. Not wanting to drink is different from wanting not to drink. Not wanting to drink requires no willpower. I don't want to drink, in the same way that I didn't want to drink when I was ten.

I wanted to drink in my twenties – a moderate amount, and often slightly more than a moderate amount. In those days I went through periods of wanting to drink, and periods of not wanting to drink. And then something happened at the age of thirty-two. The periods of not wanting to drink disappeared. I drank more and more, and snorted cocaine more and more, and stayed up late, and woke up late. I wrote for glossy magazines. I wanted to write memoirs. In my twenties, I would spend a few hours a day writing articles for glossy magazines, and maybe three hours a day reading books, and studying the books, trying to understand the techniques the writers were using, and then making notes. When the drink took over, in my thirties, I would write articles for glossy magazines, but I would always have a hangover, which shortened my working day, and working in the evening was out of the question, because I had to go out and get drunk.

My drinking was eating away at my mind, at my work, at my career, at my life, and on one level I knew this, but I really didn't want to think about it; the knowledge existed as dark shadows somewhere deep in my brain. And of course I didn't want to think about the dark shadows, they are a sort of illness, and of course there is a remedy for this illness, and of course the remedy comes in a bottle, and of course it makes the dark shadows get bigger, and of course there is a remedy for when the dark shadows get bigger, and of course it comes in a bottle.

It was as if I was at a party, and a lot of people I knew, the people who wanted to get married and have children – the people who wanted to have a life – were leaving the party, or had already left the party. One of the things I did not want to confront was the fact that I was not, nor did I feel I could be, or wanted to be, or maybe even deserved to be, in the group of people who had left the party.

This, I told my therapist, was because I could not imagine, I *could not imagine* what it would be like to leave the party, to leave the party and have a life, to leave the party and live in a house and create a little world; I could not imagine how I could create a little world.

'Why not?'

I pondered this. 'Why not? Because I would spend all my time thinking it was going to disappear. I would spend all my time thinking that someone would take me aside, and tell me that my little world was about to disappear.'

Father Greg and Father Craig

It's 1975. My mother tells me to sit down. For a while, she talks about lakes and beaches. She talks about swimming and house-hunting. We will swim. We will hunt for a house. We will stay on an island. We will have fun. Of course, there is a catch.

We fly to Halifax, Nova Scotia, and then we get into a much smaller plane and fly to Sydney. Sydney is on an island. We get into a taxi and drive on a highway and after half an hour we're in a street of low detached wooden houses. We have rented one of these houses. It belongs to a football coach, so there are trophies, and pictures of boys in team shirts. Behind the house is not exactly a garden, but lots of empty grassland with trees in the distance. There is no sign of my father.

Later, there is a knock at the door. It's two men, dressed in jeans and checked shirts. They introduce themselves as Father Greg and Father Craig. They are carrying a wooden box, and when I ask what's in the box, one of them says 'lobster'.

Father Greg and Father Craig walk down the hall and into the kitchen. One of them takes a pot from a cupboard and fills it with water. He lights the stove. He says, in an accent that is not quite Irish, something about welcoming us to Cape Breton. That's the name of the island.

When the water boils, Father Greg or Father Craig – they are Catholic priests – opens the box. Inside, alive, are the lobsters. Maybe a dozen of them. The two priests drop the lobsters into the water, a few at a time. One of the priests unfolds a newspaper and flattens it on the kitchen table. When my father arrives, about an hour later, we have eaten most of the lobsters. He is wearing a lightweight suit and a knitted tie.

House Hunting

The next morning a few kids were throwing a baseball around in the grassy area behind the houses. My mother suggested the idea of going outside to meet them. They were pretty friendly. As in St John's, they spat a lot more than the kids I knew. I could now see there were low walls suggesting the shape of gardens, but no more than suggesting. Some kids were sitting on a wall and drooling down between their feet.

A guy came up to me. He was about my age. 'Brett,' he said. Finally I said, 'Uh, Will.' We stood around for a while.

'Hey, Will,' said Brett. 'Would you be ready for some tree shittin'?'

He explained it to me. In the distance, where the trees were, was a particular tree. The idea was to climb this tree, and sit on a particular branch. Someone would fashion a target on the ground. You had to aim just right.

'This guy, Ricky Rotherham,' said Brett, pointing at a smaller, thinner boy. 'This guy, whoo-hoo!'

There had been some kind of triumph the day before – a bull's eye. Ricky had inched his way along the branch. He'd slid his trousers down. His aim had been true.

You had to make sure not to empty your bowels in the morning.

'Are you in?'

I went back to my bedroom and listened to *Dark Side of the Moon* by Pink Floyd. Later, my parents drove to a lake somebody had recommended – Blacketts Lake. When we got there it was deserted. My mother thought we must have got the wrong place.

We hadn't.

There were hundreds of lakes. They had these tiny little beaches. I found a little beach and took off my jacket and made it into a pillow. I lay down and turned on my cassette recorder and listened to Pink Floyd. My father said: 'I hope that's a mind-blowing experience you're having.'

There was a college on the island, and my father had a job at the college. They had agreed to his comings and goings. This part of his life would be very active in the next few years – he would go to Russia, Kenya, Nigeria, East Germany. The college was tiny. There were some buildings, and some prefabricated buildings. My father's job title was 'Dean of Arts and Science'.

Sometimes my father spent part of the day with us, and sometimes he didn't. It was a summer of swimming and driving around and looking at houses. For weeks, none of the houses we looked at were right. My mother didn't like them. They were big enough. But not right. They would be a boxy, wooden house, in a line of boxy wooden houses, with big spaces in between.

My father had arranged to meet an American guy named Donald who lived an isolated life on the edge of the wilderness. He owned some land – some fields and a few hills with a creek at the foot of the hills and a forest on the other side of the creek.

Donald let me drive one of his tractors. I drove it down a hill, and let it get out of control, and for a couple of seconds, as it decided whether or not it would tip over, I was looking at a different life from the one I ended up having.

There was an old guy two houses along from the one we were renting, a World War Two veteran who lived alone; he had a gym in his basement and he let the local kids use it. He had a cigarette-rolling machine and he let the kids use that, too. There were girls, but I just talked to them. Nothing happened. I read novels by Jacqueline Susann, Rona Jaffe, and Jackie Collins – the house had a lot of books about women who yearned for the right man to come along and straight up have sex with them. I thought about what I'd be doing when the summer was over. For instance, how did masturbation work in a dormitory? The last time I was in a dormitory I'd been eleven, and I couldn't remember.

One day we found the right house. It was up a hill, in a wood, above a river. It had balconies. It had a sunken sitting room and deep carpets. The fireplace was made out of huge rocks. This was the house my parents would live in. In a few days, my brother and I would fly back to England, to boarding school, with my mother. My father would fly to Moscow. My mother would fly back to the new house. But when she arrived my father wasn't there. He did not call. Days went by. People kept calling, wondering where he was. Eventually he arrived at the house, having been missing for ten days.

He would never talk about those ten days.

Sydney River

A hot day at the end of the summer. We are driving along. On the days my father is around, we do a lot of driving. We pass a sign with two names on it. The sign says 'Sydney River', and below that it says 'Glace Bay'. In a low, expressionless voice, I intone the words: 'Sydney River, Glace Bay.'

My brother laughs. About a minute later I do it again.

'All right, that's enough,' says my mother.

My father is hunched over the wheel. My mother says: 'I think you've missed the turn.'

'I have not missed the turn.'

'I think you have.'

I say: 'Sydney River, Glace Bay' in a singsong voice. My brother laughs.

My mother says: 'No, you really have missed the turn.'

My father stares ahead. The road is a straight line to the horizon.

I say: 'Sydney River, Glace Bay.'

My mother says: 'Could you please *not* do that!'

She turns to my father and says: 'For God's sake! You missed the turn! The turn was back there!'

'Sydney River—'

My father steps on the brake. The car lurches. He unclips his seat belt. Air rasps in his throat. He opens the door. Gets out and starts to walk away from the car. Does not close the door.

I watch as he gets smaller and smaller. I am appalled and excited. Later – after he turns around, after he walks back to the car – we drive past lakes and more lakes. We find a perfect sandy beach.

Lakes and beaches. Of course, there is a catch. As a family, we will be living thousands of miles apart. That's the catch. My childhood has ended. There won't be any more of it. That's the catch.

An Act of Violation

I am sitting on my sofa, reading Karl Ove Knausgaard. He's talking about the first time he saw his father's dead body. He says it looks wooden, like it's been carved. Looking at his dead father, he says, 'feels like an act of violation'.

When somebody dies, we try to forget the body – how the body makes us feel. We try to remember the living person. Not the rotting person. This idea is so creepy that I put the book down and look around the room, my friendly sitting room, and I wonder if there has ever been a dead body in this room.

And a memory springs into my mind, a memory that's actually about forgetting dead bodies. It is the only time I can remember my father intuiting my feelings.

The only time.

I was twenty-seven. He was sixty. I was living in London. He was living in Canada, but was visiting my mother, who must have been living in England at that time. After the first few years, she lived in Canada less and less. The night before, I'd seen a horrific thing.

I was walking along a street. There were blue flashing lights in the distance. A man ran up to me in a policeman's uniform. He was crying. He bent over a wall and vomited. I kept on walking. Then I saw the thing. The things. Later, I could not understand how the things were wiped from my mind. But they were. The next day, I sat on my bed all day, feeling very weird, not quite depressed, but disconnected. Time moved very slowly, but when I looked at the time, hours had passed.

I got on a train and looked out of the window, not quite aware of where I was going, not able to focus. I got off at the stop nearest my parents' house. I called their number. My father met me at the station.

'What's happened? You look terrible,' he said. I had no idea what had happened. It was the weirdest thing. The way everything was wiped from my mind. The blue lights. The vomiting policeman. The crushed car. The body parts on the road.

That arm.

From a Distance

When Knausgaard hears about his father's death – his father was fifty-six, he drank himself to death, he had been a bully, he had gone to live in alcoholic squalor with his alcoholic mother – when the phone rings, and Knausgaard's brother tells him their father has died, Knausgaard's reaction is as follows.

During the call, he looks at himself in the mirror and notices that his own face is 'watching me from somewhere far away'.

I love that. As he writes, he is watching himself from a distance, so he is watching himself watch himself from a distance, from a distance.

Then he puts the kettle on. He looks out of the window. He stares at the kettle. He thinks about how lucky he is to live in such a nice place.

Next, he tries to understand the meaning of his father's death. But he can't. He decides that it is meaningless, and also that it is not. But it 'did not occupy the position in my consciousness that it should have done'.

He wonders if he will inherit any money, then wonders why he is thinking this thought, then tells himself he can't help thinking this thought.

He asks himself if he should masturbate, but decides not to, because his father is dead.

He calls his girlfriend. He gets a taxi to the airport. He goes to see his father's body. Looking at it 'feels like an act of violation', because he has never before been able to look at his father's face without the possibility of his father looking back at him. When he exits the chapel, he leaves the door open, because 'Even though I knew it was irrational I didn't want Dad lying there on his own.'

I really want to meet this guy. I must call him.

What He Did

I've agreed to interview David Bailey, the photographer, for a story, so I catch a train to London. At the station, 'Fairytale of New York' by the Pogues is playing. A song about falling down the rabbit hole of addiction, and hitting rock bottom, and being nostalgic for an earlier time when things were bad, but not quite so bad. In the depths of a hangover, a man remembers how much fun it was to get drunk, even if it doomed him – sort of.

It seems to me that the fun and the doom are connected.

I take a taxi across the Christmas-themed metropolis. Bailey's studio is in a mews near King's Cross. He is an old man with wispy grey hair and the dignified remnants of a pretty face. The last time I met him, he was fifty-eight. Now he's seventy-six. I think he's changed more than I have in the intervening years, going from middle-aged to old, whereas I've gone from thirty-five to fifty-three, from the tail end of not-quite-youth, what's known as 'middle youth', to the actual state of being middle-aged.

You have to take into account that I was a bad thirty-five; I am, I hope, a better fifty-three.

To look at, Bailey reminds me of someone. I sit down, and soon we're chatting away – about life, sex, relationships, women and desire.

'I like women,' he says. 'They're great.' He thinks for a long moment. 'To me, women have always had a kind of mystery. And once they lose their mystery, they lose their—'

He leaves the thought hanging.

'Men', he says, 'are all sort of, they think with their dick, whereas women's fantasies are much better than men's fantasies. Women are much smarter than men. They might not be good at climbing mountains, but they're definitely good at surviving.'

I can *see* this. People are really fascinated by women's fantasies, but not so much by men's fantasies, even though men's fantasies are mostly about women – and the female body is the world's prime aesthetic object. It's like: women's sex toys are absolutely fine, but men's are sleazy, even though men's sex toys are representations of female sex organs, and women's sex toys are plastic dicks. So women's fantasies perform some kind of miracle, turning the profane into the sacred, and men, who think with their dicks, perform a reverse miracle, turning the sacred (the female inner sanctum) into the profane. My mind alights on something I saw in a documentary, and flits back to the present.

I love talking to this guy. 'I've been lucky,' he says. 'I've had some great relationships, and I guess I'm good friends with all of them. Not bad friends with anyone. I still love Penelope Tree. I still love Catherine Deneuve. But some people you can't live with. It's not a question of whether you love them. You have to be able to live with someone. You have to be practical. It sounds boring, but you have to like being around somebody. Not just because you love them. There has to be a practical side to love for it to work.'

I ask him how many women he's slept with. What I mean is 'had sex' with. He says he doesn't know. He asks me how many I've slept with. I tell him. My number, whatever it is at the time, always sounds too big and yet too small, too small and yet too big, if that makes any sense. Probably not. But actually, it does. A small number sounds loserish; a large number sounds needy.

'Fifty-five.'

On the way back I realise who he reminds me of. It's my father. And that's not because he actually reminds me of my father. He does, a bit. But that's not the main reason, which is that I'm always seeking father figures; it's something I've always done, and always put to the back of my mind, because I associate it with shame. People I have interviewed: actors, writers, politicians, film directors. Jack Lemmon, Ernest Borgnine, Elmore Leonard, Paddy Ashdown, Francis Ford Coppola. Teachers and tutors. David Bailey. As I get older, they become more scarce.

I would never have a conversation with my father about sex. Or rather, he would never have a conversation about sex with me. Maybe because my father's mindset was formed before the sixties, and mine was formed after the sixties. Bailey, of course, provided the images for the sixties. He created images of people who seemed to be looking at you, and you could see right into them, could see they were a bit fragile and damaged. A picture of the Beatles made them look smart, attractive, hungry for something, but scared; in his famous picture of the Krays, they look aggressive and wary at the same time. He stripped a layer of fake dignity away from people. You could see the sex in them. But my father would never want to talk about how many people I'd had sex with; he would not want to be the keeper of that knowledge.

I take a seat on the train and look out of the window at the dark city. I think of all the things I have never, and will never, talk to my father about. Relationships. Sex. Dating. Men and women. Ambition. Desire. And I think of all the things I might still talk to him about. Language. How language shapes the way you think. How people develop different mindsets – left-wing mindsets, libertarian mindsets. We could talk about those things.

And about all the places he went to. But not why he went there. Or what he did.

A Lovely Christmas

I wake up on Christmas morning. My house is quiet and peaceful. I am alone. My emotions are a mixture of guilt, shame and fear. I am not with my son. I am not with the mother of my son. I am fifty-three. I will visit my parents. I will upset my mother, I'm certain, because I mostly can't hide the fact that I don't like Christmas, particularly Christmas Day, that it pushes my buttons like nothing else. Apart from maybe my birthday.

But I can hide on my birthday. I can get away from people. Christmas – no. Not possible.

I wrap my presents. I know my mother will say how well wrapped they are. She will say that, in this respect, I take after my father's father, always very precise in his physical actions, always very well dressed, and I can't help thinking, the thought just intrudes, that his two daughters died, poor things, and his wife, my grandmother – I got to know her when my parents were abroad – she said it was a gas leak, told me that her daughters, my father's not-quite-sisters, died in a gas leak, but actually, no, they did not.

I start to wrap my father's present. I always give books, and an expensive card, a Vermeer or Rembrandt.

I don't want to be too early. I turn the radio on and twiddle the dial. The Pogues: 'Fairytale of New York'. There is a minuscule shudder in my tear ducts. I think maybe the song is set at the moment of the singer's death, he's crossing the line as he loses consciousness, crossing the line as his life flashes through his mind, which might and might not be a scientific possibility, but I think that's what's happening in the song.

The tape spool. The wrapping paper. I always use proper tape dispensers, with 'invisible' tape and serrated teeth so the tape tears off cleanly. There is no mess, no searching the spool for the break in the tape, no tape twisting, no tape stuck to your fingers causing mayhem. And I always use thick, glossy paper that won't spring open when you fold it. I cut the paper to the right size, think of how I'll fold it, fold it, tighten the paper, tape the two sides together, concealing the gift, make the ends into little triangles, fold the triangles, and tape them shut. At the end it looks like a perfect little box.

I walk to my parents' house the quick way, along a major trunk road, something people don't do; in fact I remember a comedy based on a guy who needed to walk along a major trunk road every day, and the fact that he was doing this, this thing that people don't do, automatically made him a comic figure.

Cars swish past every so often, people aiming themselves at those who conceived and gave birth to them, or those they conceived and gave birth to, decades earlier, two or four people to a car, bent over instruments or gadgets, their faces blank.

I arrive. We eat. My father doesn't eat much. He usually does. Always a fiend for the meat, the gravy. Coming alive at the table. Grinding the pepper with gusto. From the Latin *gustare*, to taste. Doing something with gusto really means doing something that is to your taste, something you love. Which, in my father's case, is actually to taste things.

Or rather, was.

Today he carries himself at a sort of ironic distance, as if he is present, but also not quite. He has a half-smile. I love him. His hand, and the hand that holds his knife, are still. Next to the knife is a glass of alcohol-free beer, the surface of which is misty, with clear patches from the grip of his fingers.

Later, I present him with the book. He is sitting on a sofa. He takes the book and gets to work on the unwrapping.

My mother says: 'Lovely wrapping – just like your grandfather.' I think of him young, slim, attractive, dressed for the First World War; I think of him walking in the street with an overweight boy in the 1930s; I think of him at the very end, rummaging through a chest of drawers.

His son, the former overweight boy, finishes unwrapping and releases my gift. He looks at it.

'Ah.'

'Yes.'

'Well . . .'

'Yes?'

'Thank you.'

'Well.'

'Happy Christmas.'

'Happy Christmas.'

'Nice card,' says my mother. I had wanted to get Vermeer's *The Little Street*, so I could make a point of tucking it inside the frame of the print that hangs in the kitchen extension, next to the other versions of the same painting that have, over the years, been similarly tucked. But I had to make do with *The Music Lesson*.

Why didn't I get *The Little Street*? Why didn't I get *The Little Street* and tuck it in? The one thing I could have done.

The one thing.

My father gets up from the sofa, walks into the garden extension, and lowers himself into his favourite chair. I have missed my chance. I should have thought about this, should have planned it better.

The perfect time would have been – when?

A year ago, to the day.

So I talk to my mother instead, in the sitting room, out of my father's earshot. He's really very sick, she says. He sleeps a lot of the time. Today has been a struggle for him. The meal. And then the presents. Still, she found him sitting at the dining table a few days ago, a cardboard wallet file open in front of him, writing on pieces of paper, cutting them into strips, putting the strips into smaller wallet files.

'He makes them himself,' she says. 'He cuts things up, like brochures or magazine covers, and makes these perfect little files.'

This worries her. Perfect little files. Possibly a bad sign.

My father is now asleep in the garden room. My mother drifts into the kitchen. I could run upstairs and steal some of the opioid pills she uses for when her arthritis flares up, I could be up the stairs in no time, could be swallowing two big pills less than a minute from now, and lie here as the peaceful morbid rush laps at my brain. A bad idea.

Anyway, I'd better get going. I will talk to my father another time. It's been a good Christmas, I tell my mother on the doorstep.

A lovely Christmas.

It's Dark

The next day I pick up my son from his mother's house, and I take him to see my mother and father, and my father looks tired, very tired, and I go home with my son, and we play *Plants vs Zombies*, and we talk about *Plants vs Zombies*, and I watch an episode of *The Bridge*, and think about Scandi noir, and I cook for my son, and the day after that I take him skateboarding, and watch him for a little while, happy and amazed and maybe a little worried at how fearless he is, and after a few days I take him back to his mother's house.

On New Year's Eve, I go out, having not had a drink for more than 364 days. It occurs to me that, even though I don't want to drink, something inside my head might change, might say, come on, you've been sober for a year, you can drink just this once, maybe just on New Year's Eve itself, you could in fact drink one day in the year, every year, as a kind of tradition, but anyway, when I get to the bar, to order a round of drinks, I buy alcoholic drinks for other people, and a soft drink for myself, because I have no desire to drink, none at all, which strikes me as another turning point, and it might be the first moment when I think: I might never drink at all, ever again.

I go to see my parents. My father is quiet. I have two simultaneous pictures of what's happening to him. Either he's dwindling, very slowly, so slowly that everybody will be able to forget about it, and in the summer he'll be even quieter, even more glazed, but still walking up to his study every day to work on his words, and next Christmas he'll have even less appetite, and he'll sit in his favourite chair, in the garden extension, a ghostly presence. Or he will die. But when? Every night, when I go to bed, I put my phone on my bedside table, and look at it, and wonder if it will ring during the night.

My article, about not drinking, is published, and as always I find it difficult to read on the day of publication. But the next day, I open the magazine, and look at the picture of myself sitting on a bench by the sea, and I remember that, when the camera clicked, I was thinking about the last time I'd been photographed in almost this exact spot, to accompany an article I'd written about how time seems to speed up as you get older; I look at myself (the navy coat, the Vans shoes, the scarf I hadn't wanted to wear), and the photograph, I have to admit, is fine, or at least not bad, and I read the article, and put the magazine down, and put my phone on the bedside table, and the next thing I know, it's ringing, it's dark, and I pick up the phone, and I'm not yet awake, and I look at the phone, and on the screen it says: 'Parents'.

The Bottom of the Stairs

It's my mother. She's talking about my father. I'm still waking up. One part of my mind is grasping for details. But my mother's tone is the dominant vector of information.

The situation is very bad, says the tone.

Words and phrases she is saying: heard a noise; bottom of the stairs; called 999; he was just; he was just; he was just sitting there; they took him; they took him away; but what could I do; he wasn't himself; he was *not himself*.

I tell her I'll be right there.

Half an hour later I'm standing at the bottom of the stairs in my parents' house. My father did not fall down the stairs. At least there's that. It seems he got up in the night and walked around the house in the dark. My mother heard a noise. She came down. He was sitting at the bottom of the stairs.

He was awake. But confused.

'I tried to get him to go back upstairs,' she says.

He did not want to climb back up. So my mother settled him in his reclining chair in the garden extension. She covered him with a blanket. He fell asleep. She went upstairs. Then she fell asleep.

There was another noise. It was just after 3 a.m. Again, my mother came down the stairs. Again, my father was sitting on the second step. Again, he was confused. Again, he refused to go back upstairs. And this time, he refused to go back to the reclining chair.

He was not talking. So my mother did something she would later regret.

She called 999.

We drink a cup of coffee. The fact of my father being taken away feels very strange, even though this had to happen, it was obvious this would happen. The good news: my mother says she was told, by the paramedic, that my father would be back later today – by five o'clock. I can't imagine why he would say this, or how he would know. But it means that we have something to do – he said we must get rid of all the rugs, anything my father might trip on; we must also dismantle his bed and bring it down the stairs and put it together again in the garden extension.

But, I'm thinking. He didn't fall down the stairs. He got up and walked around, and sat at the bottom of the stairs. Then he went to sleep. Then he got up again, and walked around again, and sat at the bottom of the stairs again. Maybe this has happened before. Maybe he's been doing it for a while, and my mother hasn't noticed.

Also: he's always very careful when he goes up or down the stairs. Plus he no longer drinks.

And now something occurs to me: I can go into his study, while he is out of the house, under the guise of dismantling his bed. My brother is coming in a few hours to help. But I can go into the study.

Nobody will stop me.

I finish my coffee and go upstairs and stand outside the door. There is a bolt on the door; he fitted it years ago. As a means of stopping people from getting in, it's useless. It's the sort of thing you might put on a stable door, to stop a horse getting out. But still, the bolt does its job. It's performative. It says: keep out! It creates a sense of taboo.

Anyway, the door is not bolted. He must have pushed it open at midnight, thinking he'd be back in a minute.

I go through the facts. He wakes up. He goes down the stairs. Maybe he wants a cup of tea. Maybe he's looking for a book. But at some point, he loses the thread of what he's doing. So he walks around in the dark. Makes a noise. On the way back, he sits at the bottom of the stairs. Maybe he's trying to remember why he came down in the first place. When my mother finds him, he is confused. He does not want to go back upstairs, and doesn't seem to be himself.

He's half asleep. He's unwell. He's at the bottom of the stairs, trying to remember something before he goes back upstairs, and by the time my mother finds him, the thing he's trying to remember has retreated further into the distance; now he's trying to remember the state of trying to remember the thing he was trying to remember.

So he agrees, not to go back upstairs, but only to go as far as the recliner in the garden extension while he tries to remember what he was trying to remember, which is: why did he come downstairs? And he falls asleep, and wakes up three hours later, in the recliner, the place he'd normally find himself when he wakes up from his afternoon nap. But the fact that it's the middle of the night confuses him. Half asleep, he wanders back through the kitchen and resumes his position at the bottom of the stairs, trying to think his way out of his confusion.

Like the South African philosopher, whose landlady was surprised that he liked to sit in an armchair for hours and just think, whose name I now remember: J. N. Findlay, the man who supervised my father's master's dissertation, the title of which was 'The Philosophy of Psychology'.

That's when my mother came down the stairs a second time. That's when she called the emergency services. Hence the paramedic. Hence the paramedic's instructions. Hence the fact that I am now standing outside the door to my father's study. I am here to look at the bed. At this point, I really don't think we will end up moving the bed at all. My father might well come back this afternoon and nix the plan.

I open the door and walk into the study.

I wonder if my father has any sense, whatever he's doing in the hospital, or is being done to him, that this might be happening, that I, his son, am trespassing.

He is on a bed, being injected by a nurse – maybe. He is booking an ambulance to take him back home – maybe. He's already on his way – maybe. The ambulance is slowing down. He will be outside the house in a few moments – maybe.

I'm *in* his *study*. There's a bed on one side of the room. There are two chests of drawers – the one that they've always had, and the one that arrived in 1992, when my grandmother died, the Victorian one my grandfather ransacked in 1977, the one that my father was ransacking two weeks ago. When my mother found him doing that, he was sleepy and confused. That was in the middle of the day. What happened last night – being confused in the dead of night – was actually *less odd* than that.

So why call an ambulance?

Because it was the middle of the night, and things always seem worse in the middle of the night. Or possibly something was deeply wrong – he was *not himself* – and my mother just knew.

I can hear her moving around downstairs.

There are clothes in a jumble on the floor by the bed, and an A4 wallet file, open, its contents spilling out. Inside this file, there are several – six! – miniature files, the ones he makes himself, and inside these miniature files are sheets of A4 paper, cut in half, covered in tiny, neat handwriting, and pinned together by paperclips.

On the outside of the file, he has drawn a diagram, like a family tree, the patriarch being Proto-German, with its successors Old High German, Old Saxon and Old Dutch, and each of these has offshoots – German Yiddish, Low German, Dutch Afrikaans. The files on the inside have their own subjects. One says: West Germanic, Anglo-Frisian, Old English. Another is: Icelandic, Faroese, Norwegian, Danish, Swedish.

These might have been the subjects of his last thoughts, before he turned the lights out and fell asleep.

There's a built-in wardrobe, six feet wide, and I open it, and – wow!

Dozens of A4 wallet files, stacked neatly, each labelled on the outside, each filled with the smaller, home-made files. I pick a file from the top. This file covers slang words from the West Riding of Yorkshire, collated in 1781: addle, arr, attercop, beck, beild, ber, dannet. Meaning: earn, scar, spider, brook, shelter, the space a person runs in order to leap, a bad person.

Another file focuses on the *Cursor Mundi*, a poem in Middle English from the early fourteenth century. Yet another is material on the Harley Lyrics, written in Middle English and Anglo-Norman, also in the fourteenth century.

My mother calls up the stairs.

I put the files back. I close the wardrobe. I open the middle drawer of the Victorian chest of drawers; again, several A4 files. But older, battered, with coffee stains, the edges reinforced with ancient Sellotape.

Inside the top file is a document that says:

United Nations Educational, Scientific and Cultural Organisation
Seminar on Programmed Instruction
Varna, Bulgaria, 19–29 August 1968
Final Report

I take this file, tuck it under my arm, close the drawer, leave the room, walk into the room that used to be my bedroom, put the file on top of the chest of drawers, leave the room, close the door and walk downstairs.

Later, my brother appears. He looks as scruffy as me, and smells of alcohol – although so what, because I have become very sensitive to the smell of alcohol. Lots of people smell of alcohol. My brother's alcohol smell is layered – it goes back in time; he's been drinking every day for a little while. But then again, I must have been worse, until very recently – just over a year ago.

Drinkers can't smell drinkers. Teetotallers can. Two different worlds.

I don't think we should move the bed. Everybody else does.

My brother and I dismantle the bed, take it downstairs in pieces and reconstruct it in the garden extension. Normally, I refuse to do any of this kind of work, in case it damages my back, and it occurs to me that maybe I don't want to move the bed simply because it suits me not to, rather than for the nuanced reasons I have assembled in my mind, but this is not the time, I can see, to press my case. Afterwards, my back is fine. So maybe if I did more of this kind of thing, my back would get stronger.

Whenever I am in close proximity to my brother, it feels like there is something unresolved between us. It's our childhood, of course, and what I did to him. My mother had a word for it. She called it 'aggravation'.

'Do *not* aggravate him.'

'Now, I want you two to be on your best behaviour – and don't even *think* of aggravating him.'

But I would. It was addictive. I wanted to make him lose his temper by doing as little as possible – a tiny spark creating a huge explosion. If you saw our relationship in action, if you watched this process of aggravation, you'd say something had gone very badly wrong in my life.

We catch a bus which takes us dangerously close to our boarding school, which in turn is very close to the hospital, two Victorian campuses practically next to each other. One has money pouring into it, a constant stream of money; it's a place of well-kept lawns and carefully tended hedges; the other is starved of money. One is full of the corporate titans of the future; the other is full of junkies and sick old people. This is what I'm thinking as

I walk up the road as dusk falls, whipped by the January wind, with my *brother*, of all people.

Two facades, both built in the 1800s, I'm thinking. Life's door and death's door, I'm thinking. I very much do not want to enter, or even look at, either building. This whole place gives me the creeps.

The plan is to go into the hospital, locate our father and bring him back. Go to the ward, be brisk, be authoritative. Get a lift back in an ambulance – which will be fun. Of course, they won't put the siren on. But still. We'll get back in the early evening. My father will want his bed taken back upstairs, I bet. My back, I will say. I felt a twinge, I will say.

In and out. Get him. Bring him back.

The hospital is a very uneasy mixture of old and not-quite-new; bits are crumbling, other bits in bad taste and also beginning to fall apart. Things are at odd angles. The lobby could be taken apart and rebuilt in an art gallery by Damien Hirst; it would hit *exactly* the right note. As we move further into the building, the route we have been told to take makes no sense. We go along, and up, and down, and further down, into the bowels. A ward has been fashioned from what must be a former basement store room. The scene is like one of those pictures you see in the Sunday supplements: a makeshift sick bay in a bombed-out city in Iraq or Syria.

Our father's bed is at the far end of the ward. When we arrive, he's not in the bed.

He's behind a modesty curtain; I grasp that he's being encouraged to perform a bodily function. A nurse, male, is coaxing him along. There is a gap in the curtain; I can see the side of his face. I think he does not look happy, but I might be projecting. *I* would not be happy in this situation. (A memory, of me bursting into a bathroom in the 1970s, enters and exits my mind; my father was in there, cleaning his teeth, and told me off; I can hear his exact words: 'You didn't know what I was doing! I could have been *straining* or *wiping*!')

Straining or wiping.

Why is this person coaxing him towards a bodily function anyway, when he's about to get in an ambulance and go home?

I walk up to the desk to sort out the arrangements. The woman behind the desk refers me to a doctor. The doctor is holding a clipboard and won't stand still to talk to me. So I walk alongside him, past beds, past trolleys, while he looks through his notes. My father, he says, is not leaving the hospital today. He needs more treatment.

'He has . . . a urinary tract infection.'

'Why would he have a urinary tract infection?'

'He needs to stay here. We are treating him with antibiotics. We'll keep an eye on him.'

'Can we pick him up tomorrow?'

'I can't say. All things considered, I doubt it.'

My brother is sitting in a chair by my father's bed. My father is sitting up in the bed. He is wearing a gown and holding a cardboard receptacle, in case he needs to be sick.

Looking at it makes me want to be sick.

But he's bright and perky. Not the person he was at the bottom of the stairs. He looks much younger. He says he doesn't want to be here, that the doctors are erring on the side of caution. He asks if I will bring my mother in to see him in the morning. I tell him I'll drive her in. (She will only drive along certain familiar routes.) I take pictures of my father with my phone. He has not looked this good for ages. He has not been as focused, as vital, as this for ages. (He never will be again.)

He will be fully *compos mentis* for about another seventy hours, when his mind will be overtaken by a heavy torpor. But now I look into his eyes, and at the smile that twitches the corners of his mouth, and crinkles the skin around his cheekbones. There is a bond. There is definitely a bond. I put my hands on his shoulders. We'll have our conversation, I'm thinking.

We'll have our conversation when he gets out.

In the nearest pub, my brother drinks beer. I drink coffee. We call our mother. I look at my brother's left hand, where I broke his finger to stop him punching me in the face. He has a crooked finger, but that's better than the crooked nose I would have had, if I hadn't broken his finger.

We talk about our father's prospects with guarded optimism. Part of us collectively believes he might come home. Part of us knows he won't. My brother walks back to his flat. I get a taxi to see my mother. I talk to her for an hour, telling her every detail. I keep returning to the same phrase.

'He was himself,' I say.

I go into the kitchen, get a supermarket carrier bag, go upstairs, then into my old bedroom; I take the file from on top of the chest of drawers, put the file in the bag, and drive home in my mother's car; I put the file on the desk in my study, place my phone on my bedside table, and when I wake up, eight hours later, my phone is ringing. The screen says: 'Parents'.

Blue Badge

I drive along the trunk road and pick up my mother and then drive my mother to the hospital. I hate her car. But I don't say anything. I drive along, grinding the gears, while she asks me questions about my father.

'Was he really acting like himself?'

'Yes. He looked pretty good.'

'But why would they say he had a urinary – what did they say?'

'A urinary tract infection. Probably because he's infected all over the place.'

'But a urinary infection?'

I drive up a hill and down the other side, past a bread factory, a racecourse, a housing estate. I drive past the front entrance of my boarding school, a place that often appears in my dreams – nightmares, actually. The little tower and the slogan in ancient Greek embossed on the wall and the snatched view of the lawns and the trim avenue of trees; it makes me want to smoke a cigarette and sniff some glue. It makes me feel angry, toxic and berserk.

'Your school,' says my mother.

I drive past the hospital and up the hill towards the side entrance. I drop my mother at the entrance, a pair of sliding doors, and drive away from the hospital to look for a parking space.

I turn right and then left, patrolling the streets around my school. There are no parking spaces, unless you have a blue badge on your car signifying that you, or the person you're driving, is disabled. And then I realise – the car I'm driving *does* have a blue badge, because recently my father has been registered as disabled.

Does it count if you're driving to *see* a disabled person? Probably not. On the other hand, I think there is some chance – not much, but some – that I'll be driving him back home today. So I'm potentially in the act of driving a disabled person, even though I believe that I'm not in the act of driving a disabled person.

So technically, I'm thinking as I pull into the disabled parking space in front of a terrace of tall Victorian townhouses, I'm not breaking the law at all. The moral dimension, however, is more nuanced. What would Dr Khan do in this situation?

Sometimes I talk to Dr Khan in my head, when I'm faced with an issue of ethics. He would say: 'The rules are pretty clear. Either you are, or you are not, driving a disabled person.'

'Yes, but what if I think I might be *about* to drive a disabled person?'

'On the balance of probability, are you about to drive a disabled person?

'No.'

'Well then, using this parking space is unethical. You might be – you probably are, in fact – preventing an actual disabled person from using it.'

'Yes, but – what if the *hope* that I'm about to drive a disabled person overwhelms the rational part of my brain? If the hope is strong enough, then surely . . .'

I leave Dr Khan in a dark corner of my mind, and exit the car. Another man gets out of another car a few yards away. He looks at me, and I walk away, towards the school, towards the hospital.

The school. Memories flicker in my mind, pictures and emotions I usually try to shut down – me being whipped with a car aerial, me stabbing someone's arm with a Phillips screwdriver, a fist smacking me in the jaw, a perfect punch, me going down like – well, just collapsing in my own footprints. Me throwing hot coffee into a face; me pulling a boy's hair out by the roots. A guy taking a run-up, trying to kick me in the bottom; me spotting his run, jinking aside, catching his leg and conveying him into the air, a balletic movement, one of the best few seconds of my life, my would-be kicker landing on the back of his head as boys clapped; me being exposed to, and threatened by, erect penises, dick after dick – long dicks and short dicks, thin dicks, thick dicks, dicks aimed at your eye, dicks pissing out of windows, a dick being masturbated above my face. And boils: boils on backs, on faces. A boil exploding as a boy's head is slammed in a door. The time I thought they were going to rape me, but it was a prank, because I was new. It was a way of welcoming me. 'Welcome to the house! I bet you're disappointed, you homo!'

If I turned my head back and to the left, I would be looking at my old boarding house, would be looking at the windows behind some of which I stood, and fell, received and delivered punches, listened to Pink Floyd and the Rolling Stones and Deep Purple on expensive hi-fi systems; listened to the Sweet and Gary Glitter and Frankie Valli and the Four Seasons and Maxine Nightingale on cheap little radios; and smoked, and drank, and sniffed solvents, and hid bottles of drink in lavatory cisterns; and tried not to cry, and cried, and looked at calendars, trying to wish time away.

People keep saying to me: 'The school's much better now. That stuff doesn't happen these days.' I'm sure that, by and large, they're right.

I don't turn my head. I keep on walking towards the hospital.

My father is in a new ward, much nicer; a small dormitory with six beds. Light is streaming through a big window. Thank God, I'm thinking, thank God my mother didn't see him in the other ward. She'd have been horrified. I don't know what she'd have done. Tried to drag him out of there, probably.

He's sitting up in bed, wearing the pyjamas she has brought. She's also bought fruit, and other snacks, and alcohol-free beer, which he's already been told he's not allowed to drink, because it falls into the category of 'beer'.

He's sleepy-looking but coherent. Not as bright as he was yesterday – but, frankly, better than usual. None of us know this, but a battle is raging beneath his skin, in which billions of bacteria are destroying his organs, and billions more are marching into the big guns of the antibiotics he's been pumped full of.

'You found a parking space OK?' That's my mother.

'Yes. I just used the blue badge.'

My father, eyes narrowed, turns his head towards me.

'You parked in a disabled spot?'

'Well, I used the blue badge. So I'm entitled to.' Of course, that's not what Dr Khan said when I consulted him in my head – he said I was *not* entitled to park in a disabled spot.

'You're not disabled,' says my father. 'And you're not driving a disabled person. So you've just broken the law.'

'Maybe. But – I thought I might be picking you up.'

'You'd better go back and park it somewhere else.'

'Yes, but when I parked it, I thought I was not breaking the law. It's a grey area.'

My father looks at my mother. 'He needs to go back and get the car,' he says.

This is the last proper conversation I will ever have with my father.

A little while later, when I pick my mother up, she tells me she is horrified at the state of the ward he's in.

It's appalling,' she says. 'He can't be in there! We have to get him out.'

'We can't get him out.'

I drive out of the hospital grounds, and down the hill, and turn right. I drive past the entrance to the hospital, and past the entrance to the school, and keep on driving.

The Bulgaria File

The next day I make myself a cup of coffee and flip through the file I took from my father's study. My brother is going to see my father in the hospital today. He will call me when he comes out.

I open the file and look through the contents. There's a document reporting on the Bulgarian seminar, and lots of letters and copies of letters, sent to or by my father to various psychologists, or to the UNESCO headquarters in Paris. There's a transcript of an interview with my father, on UNESCO Radio, in the series 'Man and His Brain: a series of conversations with leading scientists engaged on brain research'.

The Bulgaria file is a detailed report, perhaps 10,000 words long, of a ten-day seminar held in the coastal town of Varna, in August 1968. My father went to Bulgaria twice, I think – my mother said he was stuck there once, couldn't get back because of some military situation.

I flip through the file. It's very dense, very technical. There are thirty-one psychologists participating in the seminar, as well as seven observers. There is a 'reception given by the Bulgarian minister of education', who is referred to as 'Mr Ganev'. The psychologists are from Poland, France, Hungary, Ukraine, Yugoslavia, Belgium, Bulgaria, Switzerland, Holland, Germany, the United States and the Soviet Union. Oddly, all Soviet names and place names and titles are rendered in Cyrillic script.

The German representative is Karl-Heinz!

And now, looking at the names, I recognise some more of them, from my father's Villa Fatima years, when we saw him in Swiss and German hotels. And, of course, French ones. So I would have met at least a few of these guys as a kid. These were his colleagues, the psychologists who went to different parts of the world, year after year, funded by the United Nations, and talked to each other – about what?

According to the report, in the Bulgarian summer of 1968, they talked about the science of conveying ideas into people's minds, and making those ideas stick. But which ideas? They were particularly concerned with science and technology, areas that were moving insanely fast in the 1960s. And computers. Soon, they believed, computers would be a key part of the education process. My father talked about tailoring education to the individual mind, in order that he or she is not just learning what to think, but also how to think. Which is interesting, because that's what I've always thought is the main problem with education. Yes, they teach you about battles and kings. But do they teach you how to think clearly?

Bulgaria, 1968. A cold war between communism and capitalism has established itself around the world. The United Nations has a project to intervene in the way people are educated. They have hired specialists. My father is one of the specialists. Some of the specialists are from the Soviet Union; others are from the United States.

The Americans don't want education to tilt leftwards. The Russians don't want it to be too far to the right. Everybody else thinks they know how to turn the dial so it rests in exactly the right place. My father thinks that place should be – where? Somewhere in the middle, I guess.

I'm checking out the other thing – the thing about getting stuck in Bulgaria – when my phone starts ringing. Did my father get stuck in Bulgaria in 1968?

I pick up my phone. The screen says: 'San'.

A Sort of Rage

A day in the early 1970s.

I'm twelve.

I'm in my parents' house reading a war comic. The comic is a 'Commando book' – an illustrated war cartoon, set in the Pacific theatre of World War Two.

Unusually, my father is in the house. My brother, who is eight, is sitting on the sofa, also reading a war comic.

My father walks into the room. This is when I make my mistake. I say: 'Look at this. This Japanese soldier calls this other soldier Major San. And then he calls somebody else Colonel San. I mean, what are the chances that they both have the same name?'

My father: 'Well, it just means sir. Yes, sir, no, sir. Major sir. Colonel sir.'

My brother says: 'You didn't know that? Ha! You didn't even know that!'

My father goes upstairs to his study.

I say to my brother: 'No, that was you – *you* didn't know that *san* means sir in Japanese.'

'Shut up. It was *you*.'

'Well, I'm going to *tell* everybody it was you.'

'But it was you.'

'But I will tell people it's you. And now you have a new name. I'm going to call you Major San.'

My brother's little face crumples. He runs upstairs. The sobbing has begun.

For a brief moment, I am filled with joy, which is quickly followed by guilt, which itself is quickly followed by a sort of rage.

The Place of Death

Four decades later, I answer my phone.

My brother says he's been to the hospital.

'It was pretty weird,' he says. 'I'm going to see Mum. I'll see you there.'

At my parents' house, my brother is talking about his hospital visit. My father has been moved to a new ward – a horrible place, my brother says. It looked like 'the end of the line'.

A place of no hope – of death, in fact. When my brother sat down next to my father's bed, my father started talking to him in French.

This is the conversation they had.

My father:	Cet homme là-bas, il est espagnol. Mais il ne parle pas français. J'ai un couteau pour moi . . .
My brother:	A knife?
My father:	Gardez le silence! Il faut parler seulement en français.

My brother: Ah oui. Je comprends.

My father: L'espagnol par là . . . Il comprend l'anglais. Mais il ne parle pas français. Oui? Cet homme, il a le désir de me tuer.

My brother: Non!

My father: Oui. C'est vrai.

My brother: Pourquoi?

My father: Je ne sais pas. La chose importante c'est. . . je dois m'échapper. Maintenant.'

My brother: Maintenant?

My father: Oui, bien sûr! J'ai un couteau pour moi. Et ici, un autre . . .

My father had hidden two knives. His idea was that he and my brother, armed with these knives, might be able to escape from the hospital – right now! Otherwise he was doomed, because the Spanish guy, who was the head nurse, would kill him.

My brother said he understood my father's position, but he thought it best not to move too fast. Maybe he could speak to someone.

My father was steadfast. The Spanish guy wanted him dead. He had to escape immediately. Otherwise they'd kill him.

I'm thinking I have seen this before – when my grandmother was knocked down by a car, and broke her hip, she believed she'd been kidnapped.

I'm thinking maybe my father has had a premonition of his own death.

I'm thinking he's been pumped full of drugs. I'm thinking I wish it had been me, and not my brother – I wish I had been the one to have the conversation in French.

Tomorrow we're going to the new ward.

The Good Old Days

I step out of the bus and walk across a road, and up another road, the air becoming thicker with every step, until it's like walking through clear jelly, the substance that surrounds the physical reality of my school and stops me from getting too close. The closer I get, the thicker the jelly gets. Before the school is even visible, there's a ringing in my ears, a fluttering in my stomach, a feeling of tenderness in my throat and chest, and a build-up of something (tears, I think) behind my eyes.

But I'm going to do it – going to walk right past the entrance – and keep on walking, right into the zone of my nightmares, and then beyond, towards the hospital, which emits its own jelly. But the hospital's jelly is not so thick. It will, I hope, not play tricks with my mind, not torment me, from the Latin *tormentum*, an instrument of torture, which ultimately derives from *torquere*, to twist. The school twists my mind, for sure. When I am close to it, I am not myself, but a twisted version of myself.

A question: when am I ever myself?

So here I am, walking past the windows where I went about my daily business – breakfast, dormitory inspection, chapel, lessons, break, lessons, lunch, dress up like a soldier, march around like a soldier, play squash, eat cake, shower, eat again, prep, change into pyjamas, dormitory, lights out, the fun begins. I always have these memories, prompted by flashes of songs, that conjure exact capsules of emotion, so Maxine Nightingale's 'Right Back Where We Started From', or at least the bit when she sings 'that sunny day', produces the exact feeling of being trapped, but looking back to the summer (lobsters, lakes, tree shitting) with a sense of loss. Frankie Valli and the Four Seasons' 'Who Loves You' – well, that's a bit more intense.

The entrance to the school. It's windy. Ancient Greek slogan. Lawns and trimmed hedges. A quadrangle of neat grey buildings. Wind in my face. I am twisting in the wind.

When I first started boarding at this particular school, I fixed my mind on a particular date – the first 'out' weekend, when I'd be able to spend one night away from the school. The date was 27 September. The kid I'd be staying with had written to me, telling me there was a party on the evening of that day. I focused on the 27th. I tried to imagine how happy I'd be on the 17th, with just ten days to go. I tried to imagine how happy I'd be on the 20th, or the 25th. Tried to visualise it. Having lunch on the 25th. Then having breakfast on the 26th.

Lights out on the 26th. Thinking of that.

The days came and went. And, amazingly, there I was, at teatime on the 27th, aged fifteen, in my friend's house, getting ready for the party. Wrangler jeans and a Wrangler jean jacket. Double denim. We were driven to a house. Pulled up to the house. Blinking lights behind the curtains and a muffled sound of drums. In the house, the parents were absent, or at least out of sight. We'd be picked up again at half past ten.

A table with snacks and soft drinks. Some people had brought tins of booze. We, who would both become alcoholics, had not. We moved into the biggest room and did some dancing. Nothing much happened. But then I saw this girl. This very pretty girl. I looked at her. She looked at me and then looked away again. And then I kept seeing her. I saw her in the kitchen. Once in the hallway, and then on the patio outside. We caught each other's eye.

Very soon it was getting late. Ideally, I would walk up to the girl, talk to her, perhaps we'd kiss and perhaps not. Then we might arrange something. But I had to act. It was after ten o'clock. It was quarter past ten. It was twenty past ten.

I got a fizzy drink I didn't want. I walked into one of the rooms. She was at the back of the room, sitting on the floor, on a cushion. Now was the time. A song was playing: 'Who Loves You' by Frankie Valli and the Four Seasons. Frankie sings: *When tears are in your eyes and you can't find the way . . . It's hard to make-believe you're happy when you're grey.* But he's offering a solution: *come to me*, he says, *baby you'll see.* And you believe him. He's painting a picture of a lonely, desperate person, and he's saying, just do this thing, this one thing, and you'll be OK. And the song makes you believe him. Just have faith, it's saying.

I walked to the back of the room. I looked at the girl. She looked back. The next thing would be to sit down next to her. Talk to her.

But I couldn't. I just stood there. I froze. I couldn't do anything. I froze. I just stood there. I could hear Frankie Valli. I can hear him now.

I walk fast, through the jelly, and up towards the hospital, where the jelly is thinner, and into the entrance of the hospital, along pathways of pale grey, pale blue, doors swinging away from me and back at me, turning into a long, open ward full of old people, one man so old I can't imagine how old he is, he must be a hundred, sitting in a wheelchair next to his bed, staring ahead, his face seamed and crinkling, sparse hair sticking straight up from his scalp. My father, I'm told, is in the next ward.

Before you get to the next ward, there's a little lobby, and a wall with a display of black-and-white photographs, and when you look closely, I don't suppose everybody does, but I do, you can see that some of these photographs depict piles of rubble, and people standing around the piles of rubble, and smashed and broken buildings, monochrome views of the Blitz, and some other pictures, of other things, and above the pictures are some words, and the words say 'The Good Old Days'.

And I open the door into the ward, which is south-facing with big windows, the sun is coming through the windows, getting all over the ward, in which there are eight beds, eight very old men, most of them lying supine and still – already dead, says a voice in my head, and one or two of them actually might be. The beds, as in a dormitory, have about three feet of space on either side. My father, it turns out, is still alive. My mother is at the end of his bed, talking to a doctor. My brother is sitting on a chair at my father's bedside. My father, whose eyes are open, looks stunned by something. Something has stunned him. He's not saying anything. I look at my mother. It's time for us to go. My brother gets up from the chair. I look at my father, whose eyes are now closed.

The ward at the end of the line.

Dying

The next morning I'm up pretty early, my phone has not rung in the night, I drink some coffee, I read part of a book, I make some notes, I start to tidy my study, I catch a bus to the hospital. On the bus it occurs to me that going to the hospital every day is just what I do now, it's the done thing, and there's something beyond this thought, a sort of blank space, a thought I don't think that exists as a sort of potential emotion, and I look outside the bus, at an abandoned petrol station, which is interesting, because there's a new petrol station a few miles along the trunk road, and I'm wondering if the existence of the new one, with its mini-mart and ATM, its coffee bar and heated snack area, its selection of refrigerated wines, the three brands of iced tea, the cuts of cold meat, the sandwiches – I'm wondering if you could say that the new petrol station *killed* the old one, which is the sort of thing you could find out if you were, what's the name of it, if you were I suppose a micro-economist. And then you could narrow it down, couldn't you – you could get all the statistics, all the numbers, and finally say, it was the ATM, or it was the cold chicken, those neat-looking packs of cold chicken that killed the old petrol station, which, if I crane my neck backwards, I can still see; it looks like an art object, you could take pictures of it and sell them to a gallery. I once interviewed an art collector, Janet de Botton, for a glossy magazine aimed at rich people, and she showed me some pictures she'd bought by an artist who had become very fashionable, she had an eye for what would become fashionable, and these pictures were black-and-white photographs of what looked like abandoned warehouses, very grim you might say, but they had an undeniable power, the pictures, they were making a bold something or other, not exactly statement, but there was nevertheless something bold about them.

My phone rings. It's my mother. She's trying not to cry. She says that I'd better prepare myself for this, which is that my father, she says, is dying, which comes as a relief to me, because I was sure she was about to say 'has died', the exact words she used when she told me, in 1984, that my friend Andy 'has . . . died'; and I felt that this formulation was softer than 'is dead', which gave Andy about five seconds extra, five seconds of life in my head, because I was trying to work out if there was any way that someone who 'has died' could still be alive, neurons fizzing in my brain, making the case that, surely, if Andy was dead, then that's what she'd have said, she'd have said that Andy 'is dead'.

But my father is not dead. He's alive. He's on the right side of the line. My mother is merely saying that he will die, which can be said of anybody – although, of course, my father will die in the near future, whereas I have, statistically, thirty-odd years to go.

I'm still thinking he might leave the hospital. That's what my mother was trying to arrange when she was talking to the doctor yesterday. She said she wanted him to be out of the hospital, and taken somewhere else – preferably somewhere surrounded by lawns, although she didn't actually say this, and I think what she was thinking, standing there in the ward at the end of the line, was that, if he stayed in this ward, he would die, because this was the place people came to die, some part of her mind telling her that it was the ward itself that would kill him, the fact of him being in that place – which in the end would turn out to be true.

'He's dying,' she says.

The Meeting

When I get to the hospital, my father is lying on his back, eyes closed, the skin on his face having fallen, or slipped, into a new shape, the wrong shape; he looks wrong, not peaceful, not resting, but as if tormented by some inner force – which of course is exactly right; he's being eaten from the inside by billions of tiny predators, they are eating his insides, his liver and his spleen and his pancreas and his kidneys.

He is still, definitely, alive.

My mother and my brother have arrived. We are taken into a room – a room with an old carpet, cheap wooden panelling, a large desk and three people. Seven people including us. Or rather, six. One of the people is the ward doctor. He looks slightly out of sorts, a bit furtive – but, considering what he's about to say, this might be a tic of retrospective memory on my part.

My brother and mother sit down on pale grey plastic chairs. I remain standing. The ward doctor is standing. There's a blonde woman, a junior doctor, she looks healthy and attractive, with messy hair. She's sitting on the edge of the desk. There's a dark-haired nurse. I think – I might be wrong, but I think – I appear to be the tallest person in the room, although my brother, at six foot two, would be tallest if he stood up. I have assumed a commanding posture, standing up straight, shoulders back.

I think – again, I might be wrong – that the ward doctor is addressing his comments to me.

The doctor starts to talk.

I can hear him, and I can understand his words, but luckily my brain has provided me with a lawyer, an advocate who challenges his words at every turn. The doctor says that, yesterday, my father had a round of emergency dialysis in the morning, because his kidneys had failed. This treatment raised the level of something in his blood and lowered the level of something else, therefore extending his life in this or that way. However, this morning a decision has been made not to give my father a second round of emergency dialysis, or any further rounds, because of something or other.

My inner lawyer yells 'objection!'; my inner judge hits the desk with a gavel and says: 'sustained!'

But the doctor, now in contempt of my inner court, having not explained himself properly, having put my father's life at risk, for a reason he can't explain, burbles on, guilty as sin. He's saying 'um' and 'ah' too much for my liking.

He says that we might have heard of something called the Liverpool Care Pathway, a protocol in which certain types of treatment will be permitted to the patient, and certain types won't – but that this, we'll be relieved to hear, is not what he would advise. He'd advise an entirely different protocol, which is exactly the same protocol, but different, because it's not the same at all.

My inner lawyer says: 'I rest my case.'

My inner judge says: 'Send him down.'

But the doctor carries on talking. The doctor sitting on the edge of the desk catches my eye. Is this accidental? Or is she trying to tell me something? The nurse, who is holding a clipboard, with sheets of paper furled over the top of the clipboard, looks at the writing on the paper, her eyes moving to the side.

'And so we've moved into a phase of palliative care,' says the doctor. He asks us if we agree that this is the right thing to do, and while he's in the middle of asking us, he tells us that, in his opinion, this *is* the right thing to do, we'd be doing the right thing if we agreed, and then he goes right back to asking us, and he tells us, as we look back at him, that we *are* doing the right thing, and my mother nods, and the doctor thanks everybody, and the meeting is over.

In the ward, my father is still lying on his back, looking exactly wrong, unaware of the pronouncement that has just been made, which is that everybody, the doctors and nurses, even his family, has lost faith in him, in his ability to survive, nobody at the hospital is prepared to spend any money on trying to make him better, and his family has agreed that nobody should, and on the way out of the hospital, in the bright forecourt, strafed by the January wind, her hair being blown backwards, my mother says: 'Did you understand what that doctor was saying?'

A Decision for Dr Khan

Later I pick my son up from his school, standing in the cold with the other parents, waiting for the moment when the doors open, for the roar of excitement.

My son is in a group of boys. He is eight. I take his bag. I give him something to eat. We say goodbye to people and walk down a road and across a field. On one side of us is the river. Ahead of us is the supermarket, with its alpine cupola.

I say: 'Um, we won't be going to see Granny and Grandad this weekend, because – because Grandad is very ill.'

'Is he dead?'

Children know about death, and I think deep down they fear it, maybe more than adults do, but something in their minds protects them from it. They have some idea that they're going to die, but they don't yet believe it. I remember thinking I was a member of the first generation who would experience immortality. After all, nobody had been to the moon before. If you could go to the moon – well then. Even in my twenties, I had some hope. At the very least, I thought, the picture would be substantially different when my turn came around.

For instance, every year I lived, my life expectancy would rise. At a particular moment, life expectancy would move faster than time.

Didn't happen.

When my son was three, we were walking along a path, and he said, 'Dad!'

He pointed at the ground. 'A dead bee!'

We looked at the bee. It was still. Then it started moving its legs.

'It's come back to life!'

We debated this for a while. It didn't come back to life, I said. It had been alive all along.

'How do you know?'

Well, I said, when something dies, it dies. Nothing comes back to life.

My son was disappointed.

He said: 'Where can I see dead things?'

I took him to the supermarket. I told him about the fish display. After we entered the store, he started running. When I caught up with him, he was talking to the fishmonger.

'Are they dead?' he was saying.

And: 'Are they really dead?'

And: 'They are dead.'

The fish guy said: 'I should hope so.'

'They are dead! Dad, all these fish are dead!'

I had the idea of telling him about eels – how they can die and come back to life, or at least can seem to be dead, and then seem to come back to life – I've seen it happen. But I didn't tell him about those eels.

And now five years later, he's asking me if his grandfather is dead.

'Is he dead?'

'No. But he's very ill.'

'Will he get better?'

'I don't know.'

He nods. We walk towards the supermarket.

'Dad,' he says, 'can we talk about *Plants vs Zombies*?'

At home, he plays *Plants vs Zombies* on a laptop. The next day I take him to the pool for his weekly swimming lesson. We have lunch at a pizza restaurant. Then I take him back to his mother's.

My son's mother and I have a talk at the door. I know we are estranged for a reason, but I don't know exactly what that reason is.

At the bus stop I debate my three options. I could go home; I could stay on the bus a bit longer and visit my mother, who will be back from the hospital; I could stay on the bus even longer and go to the hospital myself. Dr Khan, I think, would ask the question: where will my actions do the most good? It's between seeing my mother and seeing my father. My mother will be anxious and lonely, making cups of tea and tidying the house. My father might and might not be in a coma. I really don't want to go to the hospital. Not that dreadful place.

In the dark. Walking up that road. In that room with all those dying old men. Possibly dead old men, one or two of them, lying there. On their backs. Mouths open, flesh stretched across, the skull emerging. But imagine being my father. What if he's *not* in a coma? The worst case scenario: he's not in a coma, he's *compos mentis* but 'locked in', locked in the prison of his body, being eaten alive by billions of creatures, tiny piranhas, and he's in all sorts of pain, unable to open his eyes, just lying there, his paranoid fantasies of, what, three days ago – just three days! – having played out: they *are* trying to kill him. He is weighed down by the sense that they wanted to kill him, and he knew it, and he got the knives, and his younger son would not break him out of the hospital, so here he is, he was right all along, they wanted to do him in, here he is, in the process of being done in, and there's nobody to help him, nobody to tell, he can't even speak anyway, and how he wishes for something, a bit of company, for somebody to come along and sit next to him, so he doesn't have to do this, whatever it is, this thing, this dying, so he doesn't have to do this alone.

That's the worst case scenario. The best case: he's in a coma, unaware of his surroundings, his pain taken care of with morphine, his mind occasionally surfacing, so he feels a mixture of confusion and euphoria, he's buoyed by dreams, pleasant dreams – of the Alps, maybe, of constructing some perfect hypothesis to do with how the brain learns and unlearns, of Karl-Heinz shaking his hand, or clapping him on the back, 'Ja, Herr Professor Leith, das ist sehr wichtig!' And then standing on the balcony of some Swiss hotel, I can see it exactly, wooden, on the edge of a ski resort sort of place, it's evening, he's looking at the sharp peaks, breathing the alpine air, maybe a single whisky, he didn't drink much in those days, a single whisky and then an early night, sitting up in bed with a McBain or a Leonard or a Block. So that's the other possibility. The Swiss dream. Or the Nova Scotia dream. A day to himself, in the house in the woods, tackling the Ernest Jones biography of Freud for the second time, maybe taking his chair out onto the balcony of his study, with a view of dense pine trees, you could walk through those trees for half an hour and still not come to the end of them, although of course he never liked walking much, only did it when my mother made him do it, I suppose like lots of things. Swiss dreams, Nova Scotia dreams, floating on the morphine. On balance, I think that's more likely than the worst-case scenario. Dr Khan would say: the right choice is not necessarily the hardest choice. It's not necessarily the easiest choice either. But then would Dr Khan, who loved my mother from the vantage of his arranged marriage, and who certainly felt that my father, by always disappearing, did not show my mother enough respect – would Dr Khan be the right moral philosopher to consult on this matter?

Before the bus even comes into view, I've made up my mind.

Two Cups of Tea and a Shot of Morphine

While my mother makes me a cup of tea, I sit on the sofa in the sitting room, and I find myself looking at a black-and-white picture of my father on the mantelpiece; it's been there for years, like lots of old pictures in this house, unframed and slightly buckled, a Freudian would say this reeks of impermanence, and this might well be right.

I've looked at this picture lots of times, I was going to say countless times, but I could make an attempt at counting them, say once a week for five years, so not countless but two hundred and something times, and every time I see my father sitting on this bench, in Rapallo I think, I try to imagine him in Rapallo, sitting on a bench, taking a cigarette out of a pack, but cannot. It's the 1950s, the black-and-white era, the good old days, whatever. It's all too distant.

But today, I realise something for the first time, something to do with the fact that this is a picture of a young man, a person, with his passions, his addictions, his inner conflicts. He is *feeling* something. He's been to King's College, London, he's finished his dissertation on the philosophy of psychology; his two best friends are H. S. Eveling, whose real ambition is to become a playwright, and the young Dr Khan, whose ambition is to understand, and teach, what it is to be good. The man in the picture, my pre-father, is in the process of writing 'When to Use the Paradigm-Case Argument'. He most certainly, unequivocally, does not want children.

This is *who he is*, in this frozen moment, between taking the cigarette out of the pack, and lighting the cigarette, in the hiatus between *wanting* a nicotine rush, and *getting* a nicotine rush, the wanting being a visceral desire, a physical feeling that something's not quite right, rather than a rational thought. Soon the cigarette will be gone, the pack will be gone, the holiday will be over, and the photograph will sit in a shoe box for half a century, until my brother, always the family archivist, will find it.

I want to say, and now the photograph is buckling, while its subject lies supine, blah blah, but I very much don't want to say or even think this, and I edit the sentence as the part of my mind that forms sentences, what's it called, it has a name . . . In any case the sentence, never fully formed, fades away.

My mother appears with the tea. The ritual of a cup of tea in a difficult moment. She is tearful. This morning, she says, my father was 'quiet' – just lying there. She hates to see him like this. She has tried to get him moved, to a place with lawns, but the answer is no. The room at the end of the line represents the end of the medical establishment's patience. Moving him, says the ward doctor, would be counterproductive. I think this means the process of moving him might kill him; he might die before he even reached the lawns. He would not see the lawns. Or even smell them – which, I imagine, might well offer solace to a fading soul. But it's winter, anyway. So no dice on the olfactory benefits of mown grass.

I point to the photograph on the mantelpiece, and soon we're talking about the holidays my parents took before I was born, to the French riviera and the Italian riviera, sometimes both in one holiday, starting when my father was twenty-seven and ending when he was thirty-two, five years of going around the area between Montpellier and Rapallo, stopping in various places, swimming, taking photographs, meeting to-be-remembered eccentric characters, eating ice cream, which seemed – and probably was – particularly good, and drinking coffee, that also seemed, and also probably was, particularly good.

And that's where I used to go.

I've thought of this before, acknowledged it was weird, and moved on, but these are the places I went to in my late twenties and early thirties. Aix, Marseilles, Cannes, that place I never remember the name of that Graham Greene lived in, Nice, Monte Carlo, Ventimiglia, Chiavari, Rapallo.

On the subject of Graham Greene, I remember when, twenty-five years ago, an old friend of my father's, who had spent decades following in Greene's footsteps, tracking Greene across the globe, writing about everything Greene had done, so you could live Greene's life in real time, pretty much, if you read his book – anyway, this guy bought a house about a minute's walk from my parents' house. And it turned out this guy was not a friend of my father's, but a frenemy. There was this tension between them. And the guy kept coming round, and if I was there we'd talk about Graham Greene, and my father would go upstairs to his study, and one day I said, why don't you join in the conversation, what the Greene man was saying was interesting. When my father would go to his study, the Greene man and I would talk about Greene's characters, and their guilt, and the nature of guilt itself, which is actually pretty fascinating – it fascinates me anyway.

I said, of the Greene man, 'Don't you like him?'

My father looked at me. He took a few breaths, still looking dead ahead.

Then he said: 'I *execrate* him.'

Antibes. That's the name I'd forgotten.

I'm sipping the dregs of my tea. One summer, says my mother, my father started coughing up blood – not from his lungs, it turned out, but from his stomach. So he was actually vomiting blood. Something had burst inside him – an ulcer. He kept passing out. My mother managed to get him into a tiny French hospital run by nuns; he had a blood transfusion, and later a partial gastrectomy, after which he couldn't stand dairy products.

I pour myself more tea.

Thinking about it now, it *was* pretty weird, the way I went to all those places, at the same age as my father had been when *he* went to them. Of course, they were probably nicer places when he went to them. Monte Carlo, some people would say, was great in the fifties, and pretty dreadful by the nineties. But still, I went to the French riviera and the Italian riviera, and imagined my parents being in these exact same places.

I went to Rapallo in 1991, when I was thirty-one; walking around, I imagined my parents in the exact same places in 1959. She would have been twenty-six; he would have been thirty-two. What happened? He did not want children. She did. It was August. They had ice cream and coffee, swam in the sea, ate in restaurants, and the coffee and ice cream seemed, and probably were, particularly good, and he very much did not want children, and she very much did, and one night I was conceived, and that was that. They never went back.

Because now there was a baby to look after.

But we don't touch on this subject, of my father not wanting me, of course we don't, now is not the time; instead we talk about my father's childhood, his terrible childhood, and look at pictures of his mother and father, and pictures of his dead sisters; he was told they died in a gas leak, but that was not true.

I finish my second cup of tea, drive my mother's car back to my house, go to sleep, wake up, go to the hospital, and sit next to my father for three hours. I talk to him a bit, but not much. I can't think of what to say. But I try.

I burble on about Canada, about the priests and the lobsters, about one particular hotel in Paris, near the UNESCO building, and about how I ate too much pâté, became obsessed with pâté, and then, later, back in England, I hated it, I'd crossed some line, and now I couldn't eat it for years. I retell a story he told me about his uncles, who, like him, emigrated to Canada, and how this one uncle, Uncle Clem, ordered French fries in a restaurant in England in the 1950s, and the waiter didn't know what he meant. I talk about how my father's uncle Clem, whose name was Clement, was named after his mother, whose name was Clementina, who was herself named after *her* father, whose name was Clement. I talk about my father's uncle William, who was wounded in the trenches at the age of nineteen. Part of his head was blown off, and he came back to his parents' house in Berwick-on-Tweed, lived in his childhood home until his mother died at the age of 101, and then stayed on, amusing himself with his teenage hobbies, the collections of stamps and tools; psychologically he was always an Edwardian boy. He died in his seventies, half his skull a metal plate.

While I'm glossing over these things – I'm sure he can't really hear me – my father is moving his right hand up and down, and sometimes from side to side. The hand looks exactly like it has always looked – exactly like my right hand. For some reason, he can only move the right hand – the left one is out of sight, tucked underneath the blankets wrapped around his waist.

And then something occurs to me. Surely it won't do any harm if I try a little experiment in communication.

So I start to ask him questions and tell him to move his hand in response.

'OK, I'm going to ask you if you want morphine. If you do, put your hand straight up. Do you want morphine?'

His hand shoots up.

Jesus, he's in there!

He's in there! This is huge, and horrible, and hopeful, and a big shock; I'm tingling with guilt and horror as I talk to the nurse with the clipboard, as she signs the document and takes the document out of the ward and returns with the controlled substance and injects my father. I should ask her to inject me as well, because then we could have a sort of party, my father and I, but no, of course not. Of *course* not.

After the injection, he slumps a little, and after that, it's time for me to go.

Jesus – he's in there. At least I think he is. I might be imagining it. Part of me wants to think I'm imagining it. Part of me *hopes* I'm imagining it. But I don't think I am. I think he's in there. The idea horrifies me, and fills me with guilt, and hope, and more guilt, and more horror.

10cc

The next day I walk up the road, through the jelly, forcing my way through the jelly, a quick peek at the school entrance, lawns and hedges at dusk, I'm remembering the time when I hid in some bushes in the headmaster's garden, which is the first thing you see as you walk past, the bushes I was hiding in, that time when everything went wrong for me and my parents came back from Canada. I'd been drinking, of course, I'd been sniffing solvents, of course, but the real trigger was – was it the matron thing, or the thing when my friend was arrested, or was it both? – and my father was pacing the quadrangle, having come to get me, and he was wearing a deerstalker hat, and the sight of him was such a shock, both the sight of him and the sight of him in a deerstalker hat, that I jumped into the bushes before he could see me, and when he walked past the bushes, I tried to get his attention, and he looked around but could not see me. There was also the prank call, we did this prank call; there was also that. But I think really it was the matron thing.

Past the entrance. Through the jelly. Every few square feet of that quadrangle contains a specific memory, you could map it, if I ever hear 'The Dean and I' by 10cc, it takes me back to an exact moment, I was happy, it was when for some reason the cricket had been cancelled and we had to play football instead, and the grass had been mown, the smell of the grass was floating upwards, released by the sun.

Of course, 10cc!

Some guys at my school loved 10cc, and somebody played me all their work, made me listen to the lot, it was just brilliant, and now some of the songs make me happy and some make me sad; I would love one day to feel so happy and safe that I could sit down and listen to those songs again.

But what would make me feel happy and safe?

I push through the jelly. A world without death and disease, please. But obviously, that won't happen in my lifetime. And maybe it wouldn't be such a good thing anyway, a life without death and disease. The world would be so crowded, on account of all the people who hadn't died, so we'd have to stop having so many children; having children would be reserved for the rich. Or the clever, the very clever; you'd have to take a test, and there'd be coaching systems, like in the days of Stanley Kaplan. My father has material on Stanley Kaplan in his study, by the way. So you'd have to pay for a coach to get a top grade in the test, which would mean you could have children. And think of how attractive you'd be to women who also wanted children! You'd say, yes, actually, I got the top grade. So if I happened to get you pregnant . . .

10CC: it's the combination between Lol Creme and Kevin Godley, plus Graham Gouldman, who really is a genius, possibly one of the best ever – and, later, Eric Stewart. I went to see them when I was – what, sixteen? Seventeen? Just great. 'I'm Mandy Fly Me.'

The guy who loved 10CC had been raped, or at least sexually assaulted, by a boy I knew, and when I asked him about it, everything went blank, because I lost consciousness, because of the boy's fist, the boy who'd been raped, or at least sexually assaulted, by the boy I knew.

The jelly is less viscous as I approach the hospital, walk into the Damien Hirst environment of the lobby, along the pale blue and the pale grey walkways, up some stairs, and down a sort of ramp, sprung doors folding back towards me.

Here is the ward I have to walk through before I get to the ward at the end of the line.

Everything looks the same apart from one detail – the ancient man, with hair sticking up from his scalp, is now standing by his bed. He has got up, has got out of his wheelchair, and is standing, something I could not imagine him doing. But he's done it.

On my way past I stop and look at him. He looks back at me. Our eyes meet.

'I'm ninety-nine,' he says.

'That's . . . great,' I say.

He says: 'I'm ninety-nine! Ninety-nine!'

Across the ward, a nurse moves briskly in our direction. I move on, past the Good Old Days, past the doorway to the room where we had the meeting, and into the ward, where my father lies, not quite lifeless, on his back. He has four hours to live.

The Words

I sit down next to my father, which is to say I sit down to the right of him. There is a dying man on either side. The man next to me is different from the man who lay in this bed yesterday. Yesterday's man was supine, silent, with his mouth open, apparently breathing through his mouth, although now I see that, actually, he might not have been. Today's man is bald, on his side, his head burrowing into the blanket. Today's man twitches. He's definitely alive.

The man on the other side of my father looks dead – although, presumably, he is not, or not quite. He has arranged himself into the same posture as yesterday's man – on his back, mouth open, eyes closed, arms against his sides.

My father is, I'm pretty sure, in better shape than both of his dormitory neighbours, even though, right now, he looks comatose. Yesterday, when I went to bed, when I placed my phone on my bedside table, thinking it might ring in the night, hoping it wouldn't, I had a pang – a pang of guilt. Why hadn't I talked to my father about the thing we have in common: words? What if he dies in the night? I thought. Then I will always regret not talking to him about words, when I could have talked to him about words. Is this a selfish thought? It is. *I* want to do something so *I* don't regret not doing that thing in the future. But Dr Khan says that's OK. My attempt to avoid future regret is driven by the desire to do something that might help my father. Stick and carrot. The good person inside me sometimes uses the stick, sometimes the carrot.

So this is what I plan to do – talk to my father about words. But I have a very uneasy feeling. He's not moving. He's breathing, sure. But his hand is not moving. Maybe I missed my moment.

My window. Maybe I missed my window. From the word, I think, *vind*, meaning wind, Norwegian I think, and something else, something I don't know.

So I sit, looking at things – or rather, not things, but people, people and beds, eight beds, eight very old men. Not things, but shortly to become things, to put it crudely, people shortly to cross the line and become things. Or rather, their bodies will become things.

And then what? Nobody knows. Or do they? Science *says* it knows. Science says: and then nothing. You're done. You're not you any more. Or rather: *it* is not you any more. *It* being your remains. Although that doesn't make sense, *your* remains, because if *you* do not exist any more, then nothing can be yours – even the vehicle of flesh and bone, soon to be rotten or burned beyond recognition, that carried you through life, known as your remains. But *you* no longer exist. So nothing can belong to you. This inanimate meat belongs to somebody – but not you. Still, the language we use – *your* body, *your* remains – it's as if the very language believes in the existence of an afterlife.

And science also says, or has been saying recently, that you actually survive beyond death, in the form of brainwaves; your heart has stopped beating, your lungs have stopped breathing, usually in that order, because the failure of the heart to pump blood triggers the failure of the lungs to breathe oxygen – I think. In any case, your brain, starved of oxygen, eventually stops working. Your neurons stop firing. But neurons will fire anaerobically, for a while at least. Electrical signals will persist. It's the eel thing. Why do eels—

My father is still still. But I start talking to him anyway. I talk about the hospital, and how I've come to see him, for a chat, in this ward. Which, I say, reminds me of the time he told me that 'warden' comes from the same root as 'guardian'. To ward is to guard. And then you get those Scandinavian words – like Kierkegaard, for instance, the philosopher, and also the word for churchyard. Yard, guard. Gaard. Which means 'enclosure'. Yard, field. Enclosed area. Walled off. Fenced in. So if you meet a Scandinavian called Odegaard, it's the equivalent of 'old yard'.

My father's hand twitches. It twitches!

At least I think it does.

I say, old yard. Or old field. As in Oldfield. We have had this conversation before, my father and I. And I'm playing both parts here. The part of me, not quite making the connection between warden and guardian, between old yard and old field. And the part of him, making the connections.

I am me *and* him.

So, I say. Oldfield. (But I have got this wrong, I will realise later; old is *gammel* – so *gammel gaard. Ode* means wasted, or gone to seed.)

The hand is trembling.

For a while, I'm thinking, the hand was still. My mother has told me that it was still this morning. He was unresponsive. But yesterday, he was unresponsive in the morning. Then he started moving his hand in the evening. The days of the hand gestures. Yesterday and today. Before that, he could speak.

What were his last words? Probably nobody thought of them as last words, whatever they were, because they didn't think he'd lose the power of speech right then.

Last words – much more complicated than you'd think, because the speaker of last words can never know that these particular words or those particular words will be the last ones. If you wanted your last words to be memorable you'd need to make quotable pronouncements early in the game, and keep on making them, in case of sudden death. But that would give you another problem. When Henry James said: 'So here it is, the distinguished thing,' or when Oscar Wilde said whatever it was he said about the wallpaper, they might have later found themselves rallying, and wanting to talk, but feeling disinclined to, in case they said something bland and unquotable and *then* died. Like lots of things in life, it's a matter of timing as much as anything else.

My father's hand twitches again.

He's in there – I think he's in there, I believe he's in there, and this belief is approaching a state of knowledge. It's knocking on the door of knowledge. I could almost say: I know he's in there. And this faith feels weird. It's frightening. Knowing he's in there frightens me.

It terrifies me.

All of these thoughts hurtle through my brain – the brain is capable of having a hundred thoughts per second. And there's one thought that's very hard to think.

Which is: what is my father thinking? What is he feeling? What is it like, exactly, to be him, right at this moment?

He is submerged – literally *dipped under*. Some force is dipping him, the force of course being billions of bacteria, the attacking army of bacteria is dipping him, and I'm guessing he wants to break surface, because that would be your instinct, almost certainly. But then maybe not; maybe he wants to stay under – under meaning low, sub, sub-standard, *sub*jected to something, *sub*missive, and doesn't everybody know the upside of submission, a state in which you no longer have to make decisions, and so cannot be judged. That time I nearly drowned, on a surfers' beach, San Clemente, I was shocked to find that nearly drowning didn't feel the way I might have imagined; I was rolled around in the surf, tumbled in water, starved of oxygen, and the whole thing produced a feeling of ecstasy, ecstasy being a state in which you are outside yourself, in Latin *ex*, meaning outside, and *stasis*, meaning standing, you are standing outside yourself, in a state of rapture, which means forcefully taken, and is connected to ideas of rape, and certain creatures of prey – raptors.

Ecstasy. Rapture. Submission. That's why people drink, or take drugs, isn't it, to get into these states, the state of losing agency, of being passive, a patient, the end point being oblivion, which really means forgetfulness. That was me, until I realised that the cost of forgetting was actually too high. And now I must remember everything.

I'm thinking now might be the time to talk to my father about the time I visited him in Canada, when I was eighteen. That time in Canada. The closest we've ever been. At the time, I thought it might be the start of something.

Just before I went, I had dinner with Dr Khan. I think he knew I knew, or at least suspected, that he had feelings for my mother. When I say feelings. They were friends, Dr Khan and my mother. And we were friends – Dr Khan and me. He wasn't the sort of guy to go around seducing people's wives.

Anyway, he didn't see my father any more, and I don't think they'd said much to each other for years. But then again, my father had lost contact with H. S. Eveling, too.

He was that sort of guy, my father, always losing contact with people. As far as I knew, in terms of friendship, he still saw Karl-Heinz pretty regularly, and there was a Dutch guy he would see called Gerard, from the Villa Fatima years.

So Dr Khan invited me to dinner. He was living in London at the time, had rented a flat in Pont Street, which was pretty nice. We went for a curry. And I remember the look on his face, and the sound of his voice – he had a great sense of humour, Dr Khan. We talked about lots of things, as usual. And then he said something. I hadn't expected him to say it. I wish I could remember the exact words. He said, well, if things had turned out differently, he could have been my stepfather.

And I said that I would have loved that – that would have been superb. I'd often imagined it, actually. And then we got back to other subjects; it was a great conversation. We always had these great conversations, me and Dr Khan. I remember his face, and the tone of his voice, and how great it was to just sit there chatting, and I remember that particular day so well because it was the last time I ever saw him.

Of course I don't say any of this to my father. I take up the story in a different place, starting a few days later. Between seeing Dr Khan and getting on the plane, I lost my virginity, by the way. And the girl told one of my friends to tell me she thought she might be pregnant.

Remember that time, I say as if it had just occurred to me, remember that time I came to see you in Canada?

When was that – nineteen seventy I think nine, yes, I would say nine.

At this point, as I'm talking about the date, my father's hand moves slightly upwards; he moves his fingers as if he's tapping them on something – a keyboard, maybe.

Yes, I say, that's right – seventy-nine. It was winter, I say. So there was snow. And you picked me up at the airport. And took me to that place, I remember the name. The Ponderosa. Literally I suppose the place of heaviness – heavy steaks. The Ponderosa. That place on the highway. And they were pretty big, the steaks. And then you drove me to the house. With that sunken room. Very seventies. And that fireplace made of rocks. And those pictures of Freud.

And then, I say, I remember the next day. The streets were iced up. But you had the right tyres. You showed me the tyres.

His hand moves upwards. I take the fingers in mine, and hold it as if we were shaking hands, and I want to say something gushy, like I love you, but this might not be the exact right moment, so I say how I still remember all of this stuff, meaning about the tyres, and the Ponderosa, and the next thing I remember, which is that he drove me into town the next morning, in his Ford, with the tyres. And remember how we went to that diner, I say, and who was there? Father Greg!

I'm sounding a bit cheesy, I think, like a talk-show host, but I think this is the right tone to take. My father drove off, leaving me with Father Greg, who said this slightly odd thing, which was that there was a ship in the harbour, and he'd planned for us to get on the ship, and maybe see what it was like below deck. The first time I meet this guy, he brings a box of lobsters – and now this. And he drove me to the harbour, and we went up this gangplank, and into this ship. The inside part was a lot smaller than you'd expect, looking at it from the outside.

Meanwhile, my father was God knows where.

And then the next day, my father introduced me to this guy, I'll call him Steve. Steve was a serious stoner. He was a psychology student. We went to Steve's apartment, me and Steve, and smoked a lot of weed, very powerful stuff. And then it was one o'clock in the morning. Twelve hours – whoosh! And I had to call my father at one in the morning, and he picked up on the first ring, and sounded like this was all pretty normal. He said he'd meet me in this car park. And in this underpass next to the car park this guy was walking towards me in the dark, and I thought he was my father, and I walked up to him, but he wasn't my father, he was a janitor, he had this bucket on wheels, and he was dragging it along, this bucket, and he had a mop.

I don't say any of this to my father. I talk about other stuff. I'm the talk-show host. Talk-show hosts talk about life as if everything was very slightly surprising and totally positive. I talk about when we drove all along the big lake, the Bras d'Or, literally the arm of gold. Two of us in the Ford, the lake to our right, going on for miles.

So huge, the arm of gold. It's actually the sea, but it gives the impression of being a lake.

I talk about when we went to Montreal, a few days after this; we flew to Montreal and went out for a pizza. We made a mistake in ordering, and ordered a pizza that was far too big, and I thought he wanted a pizza that big, like for six people, and I think he might have thought I wanted a pizza that big, and we ended up trying to eat all of it, which we nearly did, and I felt pretty sick on the way home. But the next day he took me to his favourite place in Montreal, Ben's, where you could get salt beef sandwiches.

Oh, I say, and remember going to Ben's – with the salt beef sandwiches?

I wonder if he wants morphine. Maybe he wants morphine. I'll ask him.

'Do you want morphine?'

He raises his hand. Just like yesterday. And I feel relieved; I can *do* something. I can be brisk and efficient. And I'm also aware that my motivation is complex here, something I don't really want to think about. I stand up, walk up the side of the bed, exit the ward, find the nurse. The ninety-nine-year-old man is back in his wheelchair. His hair is still sticking up. Five minutes later, my father has been injected, he's definitely more drowsy now, and I'm back by the bed, staring into his face.

Getting the morphine. My complicated motivations. Like giving a child a doughnut, or a gaming console.

You want the best for them. You want the best for you. You want one thing to look like the other thing.

Now he's quieter. I ask myself some questions. Might I be making things worse? Possibly. But I am trying to make things better. Who for? Him. And me, I think. Is it possible that I'm talking to him about certain things so that I can tell other people that I've talked to him about these things? For instance, Ben's. The next time I went to Montreal, I think eleven years later, I went to Ben's, and I mentioned this fact to my parents. My father sort of smiled. But my mother – she was very enthusiastic. 'You took him to Ben's when he went to visit you,' she said to my father.

He is lying on his back, propped up by a pillow, which I think adds dignity. It gives him a very small illusion of agency. Does he know he's dying? Probably. As with Stella, I don't even hint that I might know. I am lying by omission. Dr Khan would say that's the right thing to do – without taking it too far, naturally. We have settled into the grey zone of partial denial.

I wonder about his mood. What's he feeling, right now?

As far as I could tell, his mood hardly varied, whatever was going on around him. A sort of cynicism that stopped just short of depression. A feeling that, whatever happened in the world, people would always mess things up. Driven by rogue emotions, they'd shoot each other, and bomb each other, and brainwash each other with foolish ideas. Such was life. I always wondered why he didn't get on better with the Greene man, who must have come to similar conclusions. But I think the Greene man found solace in God, which my father never did.

Trying to think about the origins of my father's gloom, I always come back to his mother. A bright, cheerful girl, she was crushed by depression in her teens when her brother died of tuberculosis, quickly followed by her mother. When her father remarried, she left home. Then she got married and had two daughters. Both died. Then she had my father, and told him his sisters had died in a gas leak. Her grief was so intense she said very little. My father's father was also a man of silence. And one day, a woman who lived a few doors down invited my father for a cup of tea, and told him the two girls had not died in a gas leak. They'd died of pneumonia, she said. Not at the same time, but years apart. And, she said, my father's parents sort of blamed each other, or maybe my grandmother blamed herself, and this guilt had been meted out on my grandfather; in any case, my father never told his mother about this conversation, which might have been driven by spite, who knows, but he told my mother, and my mother told me, but I never talked to him about it. In any case, after he left home my father hardly ever saw his parents.

And this was the baseline for my father's general mood, and this must have been why he never wanted children. He left home, he became obsessed with the question of how the brain works, a very complicated machine, and then he met my mother, the girl who danced and played netball. He must have been overwhelmed by a different version of life, which he fought against over the years, which he never stopped fighting against.

So maybe he can cope with his current situation better than one might imagine. Things are generally fucked up. Situation normal. Death is imminent. I wonder if he's been listening to what I've been saying, and if it matters, if I matter to him – a very self-centred thought. I'm inclined to think that it does matter, that I do matter to him, that I am helping, a story I keep telling myself, and will later tell others, knowing it will be helpful to them to give me the benefit of the doubt.

He didn't want anything to do with my mother's pregnancy, my father, and he didn't want to be there when I was born. He didn't see me for a week. My mother had been busy giving birth, and I'd been busy being born, and doing other stuff, we'd been staying with her parents, and then we came home. My mother handed me to my father and went off somewhere for a few minutes. When she came back he was angry. He pushed me into her. 'He was crying the whole time,' he said.

But I don't exactly blame my father for this. He was him. He had his demons. He couldn't do emotion – meaning what? He couldn't allow it. Because if emotion happened, where would it stop?

When my son was born, I was worried about what my reaction was going to be. I loved him. That was my reaction.

There was no problem.

Being a father. Nothing has made me happier. I let the emotion wash over me. It's powerful, the emotion. But my father tried to stop it. He believed he had to stop it. He did everything he could to stop it.

For my father, the alternative – not stopping the emotion – was unthinkable, because the emotion would break him down, and more emotions would get in there. Emotions about his sisters, about his mother, about his father, about being bullied, about being ill – there would be an avalanche of emotion, and he'd be buried underneath it, and he'd never recover. So he didn't want children. And when I arrived, he didn't want me.

Because of the avalanche.

Now my father is submerged, now he's actually dying. And what a thing. Who is sitting next to his bed? The baby he didn't want, now a middle-aged man, talking in the tones of a disc jockey – a disc jockey being the sort of person he hated, actually.

One evening, in 1979, in the Canadian house, the phone rang. It was for me. Afterwards I said to my father, 'Well, you're not going to be a grandfather just yet,' which was such an unexpected thing for me to say I still don't think he got it. And then he said something to me, and I wish I could remember the exact words, but it was something along the lines of his life being chaotic too. And that was that. Neither of us elaborated. The next day we went to see an Alan Alda film at the cinema. The film was *Same Time, Next Year*, in which

Alda, a married man, spends a weekend every year with this woman he's in love with – not his wife, by the way. A very emotional story. Not that Alda doesn't love his wife – he does. And not that this other woman doesn't love her husband. She does. But Alda and this woman, they have a sort of shadow life together, back in the fifties and sixties. She becomes a hippie at one point.

I decide not to mention the Alda film. Pretty soon after we saw it, maybe one or two days, my father took me to the airport and I flew off, and the next day, or possibly the day after that, he drove back to the airport and flew to Boston.

He's still breathing. But maybe his breathing is a little – what, heavier? I think that's the word. I don't think he's conscious. He might be dreaming. Of course he's an atheist. But at this moment, in the nick of time before time disappears altogether, who wouldn't be thinking about God – or St Peter? He might be just moments away from meeting St Peter. Of course he isn't. But the possibility may have crossed his mind. And what would St Peter say? He'd probably let him in. But I don't know. He should have been a better father – yes. He should have been a better husband. Definitely. Has he done enough? Have I done enough, he might be thinking. I'm pretty sure I'll be thinking that, when it's my time, even though I'm an atheist, I'm an agnostic, whatever, but at school I went to chapel three mornings a week, plus on Sundays, wearing the special chapel suit, always intoning hymns and prayers; in the House of God, it's hard to shake off, it's everywhere, so when it's my time, in the near future, very soon, the blink of an eye – when it's me I'll be wondering: did I do enough?

Maybe my father has done enough. Maybe, in that nick of time before you actually die, a sense of peace comes over you, and maybe that's because you've done enough.

For all I know, there'll be a welcoming committee – Karl-Heinz with a bowl of bratwurst, flanked by his son who died, and H. S. Eveling with a pen and a notepad and a few pertinent questions he's thought of in the meantime.

Or maybe purgatory, having to think of the same few sins, over and over. Why not turn up at your son's birth? And then why thrust him back at his mother? Why the thrusting?

I look down at him. Why the thrusting?

His breathing is definitely heavy. He breathes in – that's good. Then he breathes out. At one point, he will breathe out and not breathe in again.

Well, I say, I love you, I say, and now I've said it, but I'm not going to cry. I can tell I'm not going to cry. He wouldn't want that. I wouldn't want that. Thanks, I say. Thanks for being such a good father. Thanks for inspiring me, I say – with all the ideas, and all the words, the language – thanks for that, I say.

He moves his hand. He waggles his fingers. I hold his hand. I'm saying all these things, but other things are flashing through my mind. I keep thinking about his fingernails, how they must still be growing. Don't they keep on growing after you die? And I'm wondering what's going on in his body, underneath the blanket. I have this thought about once per minute, and dismiss it very quickly.

The kidneys. The bowels. Is there some sort of system under there?

Meanwhile I'm wittering on about books – Ed McBain, Elmore Leonard. When I was in my twenties I went to meet Leonard at his house near Detroit; we spent an afternoon and an evening together, and we talked a lot about things, about life in general. He was just beginning to be properly famous, which happened to him late in life. Another father figure for me, if only for a few hours. Of this I say not a word.

Meanwhile the man to our left, I'm pretty sure, has stopped breathing. He lies still, mouth open, mouth not moving, eyes closed. He looks – what? More than just still.

He's—

Maybe I should say something. But, actually, no. What would I say? This guy is dead? Or: this guy *looks* dead.

Maybe I was right. Now a couple of nurses are coming our way, with that briskness they have when they mean business. *They* think he's dead. Pretty soon they have pulled the curtains round his bed, and they're doing their stuff.

And then he makes this noise, the dead guy. The noise he makes is somewhere between a shriek and a moan.

It makes me jump. It should be more reassuring than alarming. But it's not. The nurses slide the curtains back again. The man looks the same. Mouth open, mouth not moving, eyes closed. He looks dead.

Anyway, if my father is about to meet St Peter, shouldn't I be managing his expectations a bit better? Listen, I should say: don't get your hopes up. Actually, if he wasn't at the point of death, I think he'd find this funny.

What I actually say is the old cheesy cliché – I tell him I love him, what an inspiration he's been to me, which might not actually be taken as a compliment, how would you feel if a drunk who threw his life away told you that you inspired him, although of course I'm not currently a drunk, and there is a small chance I might catch up on my life, so it couldn't be said that I threw it away, but I'd be asking quite a lot of my father at this exact moment to make the distinction between one version of me, the drunk who threw his life away, and the other, much more faintly etched version of me, the sober version of me, who might stay sober for a couple of decades, might start to work hard, might achieve something.

At the exact moment of his death, he might have one foot in eternity, allowing him one tiny glimpse of the future, sober me . . . but this is silly.

I love you, I say. I'm squeezing his hand.

I say, do you remember driving by the lake that time? I know I've said this before. But I've remembered something else. We're in the Ford. He's driving. I'm on the lake side of the car. The light is bouncing off the lake, so it looks less like water and more like something else, although I don't know what. A field of glare.

What I've remembered is that on the other side of the road, there's a wooden building, and my father slows down and parks by the side of this wooden building. It's a little wooden cafe. We sit at a small table and order chowder. There is a window, and outside the window is a view of a steep hill.

When we drove by the lake, I say, and you took me to this place, and we had chowder. Do you remember it – the chowder place?

I'll always remember that chowder, I say, and I squeeze his hand. Well, I love you, I say, and I squeeze his hand again.

He breathes in. Then he breathes out again. I keep getting these premonitions. I keep thinking that the breath he's taking will be his last.

I love you, I'm saying. You inspired me, I'm saying. To become a drunk and throw my life away, I'm thinking. His breathing, I'm thinking. It's not right, I'm thinking. His breathing is not right. It's dark outside, I'm thinking. It's warm in here. What happens under that blanket? Is there a system? Some kind of—

What I mean is, where does it go? But what? Where does what go? That's what I'd like to know. There has to be a system, is all I'm saying. I should have found this out. Should have—

But they've got everything taped, these people. The nurses, the doctors – masters of ceremony, I'm thinking. The curtains, I'm thinking. Those curtains.

What I'd really like to do, at this exact moment, is: I'd like to step away from this bed, just for a few moments, and go and see how Mr Ninety-Nine is doing. Is his hair still sticking up? I bet it is. That's what I'd like to do, it really is. If I had the time.

I love you, I say. I'm squeezing the hand. Then I put the hand down and squeeze the shoulder. If your life flashes in front of your eyes, like people say, how long does that process take? And that makes me think of those Hollywood people who make funeral films of somebody's life, sometimes they use actual actors, so you might have Bruce Willis playing your uncle or something. Well, maybe not Bruce Willis.

I'm sitting on the chair. I'm touching his shoulder. He's trying to breathe. Come on! You can do it! It's an uphill climb.

His neck. His chest. The hand, just like mine. But older. The face. He looks good. Actually quite good. Not like the guy on the other side – Mr Barely Alive. If that guy is alive – well, I don't know. I swear he's not breathing. You can see the shape of his skull in the mouth area. My father, on the other hand. His face. He looks good. Comparatively good.

But he's in trouble. I need to admit that now. He's having trouble breathing. And that can't be good. That *is not* good. I should do something. I have to leave the ward in twenty-five minutes. But I can't imagine my father will be alive in twenty-five minutes. I don't want to be with him when he dies. But I do want to be with him when he dies. My brain is confused. I'm entering a period of shock. I need to *do* something.

Look at him. He's in trouble.

His *neck*.

I stand up and I start to walk, first one step and then two, away from my father.

The Morning After

It's still dark when my phone rings, I'm in my bed, and here it is, the call I've dreaded, telling me my father has died. But my father has died. I already know that. So why would they be calling me? Maybe to tell me that he hasn't died, that he's not in fact dead. Maybe I should go and see him. But he's dead. But then, why would I *not* want to see him?

I could go to see him. More correctly, his body. I could spend some time with his body. The remains. The remnants. The leftovers. The bits of him that are left. Which is almost everything. When I was six or seven, already anxious about my father's regular absences, we went into a hotel. It was summer, so presumably a holiday, anyway there was a glass display case in the lobby of the hotel, and there was a stuffed lion in the display case, I can see it now, very precisely, the tawny fur and the black nose, and I said to my father, the thing is, I said, if you were to die, would you agree to be stuffed? And he thought about this for a while and said that yes, he would agree. And my mother interjected; she said this was not something that should be talked about in this way. And I said, to my father, something like: so you give me permission to stuff you, like the lion?

And now the time has come, the permission I suppose still stands, but I don't have any desire to have my father stuffed and put in a glass case. In any case, my mother would still interject.

But I have permission. But I don't *want* to have him stuffed.

I'm not yet properly awake. I pick up the phone. It's not a call. It's an alarm I set for myself a few days ago. There's an itinerary I have to follow. Second step: go to the station and catch an early train to the airport. First step: find my passport.

Here's the thing with my brain. It's not working properly. I'm in shock. I was in shock last night. Then there was all that funny business, with the nurses and the body, when I really wasn't thinking straight at all. I don't want to think about *that*. But I don't have to. In fact, I can't. I can't piece it together. The body. The nurses and the body. Me leaving the ward and then coming back, surprising the nurses, but then I suppose nothing surprises them.

After that I left the hospital. I can remember that bit. There was a taxi rank. I got in a taxi.

The driver said: 'How are you?'

I said: 'My father just died.'

'I'm sorry to hear that.'

'I mean literally. He literally just died.'

'I'm sorry. Where do you want to go?'

I said: 'What I mean is this. A few moments ago, he was alive. And then.'

And: 'I mean he literally—'

'Where do you want to go?'

'Let me think. I don't know.'

I ended up going to a pub. I went straight to the bar. I knew that, logically, people who looked at me would not know that my father had just died.

'Cappuccino,' I said.

I sat in a chair and drank my cappuccino. The woman behind the bar had sprinkled it with a lot of powdered chocolate. There was a football match on the TV. I don't think it was live. Arsenal were clinging to a narrow lead. I went to the bar again and had another cappuccino.

Then what? Then my phone started ringing and I was in bed.

My passport is in the top pocket of my wheeled suitcase. I pack a few things. At the station I wait on the platform. My father, I told the taxi driver. He literally died. Which is a fact. Eight days ago, my mother found him sitting at the bottom of the stairs. He was taken away in an ambulance. Taken to the ward at the end of the line. I tried to get him out. My mother tried to get him out.

In the airport I buy a pair of Lacoste socks. There's a reason for this, but I can't think what it is. I put the socks in my case. But then I think: what if the socks are bearers of death? Might the socks contaminate other items? Might the socks know things that the other items don't know, and therefore make the other items sad?

But no. Surely the opposite would happen. The socks are bearers of life.

He was breathing in, and I stood up. Then I walked away from him. And then something happened. But I can't remember the order of events.

On the plane I sit staring straight ahead, parts of my memory inaccessible. The journey takes about two seconds. My father has stepped into eternity. What is it that guy in Dickens says of his father? He is partaking in glory.

My father is partaking in glory.

You inspired me, I kept saying. Which isn't the brightest thing to say, if you've spent your life as a drunk who threw it all away. But then, he might have had one foot in eternity when I was saying this. So he might have had a peek at the future me – sober and productive. But what if the future me is even drunker, even more pathetic? Not a nice thought as your soul hurtles into eternity. You inspire me, says the shuffling addict.

In any case, at that exact moment it was supposed to be *his* life that was flashing before his eyes. Not mine. Was I distracting him from the main event?

And then I let his hand go.

When the plane lands I feel ultra-competent and pumped up with energy. I'm in Copenhagen. I will catch a train across the bridge into Sweden, and then

I will catch another train. Karl Ove Knausgaard will be waiting for me on the platform.

There's one tricky thing to negotiate. Do I tell Karl Ove that I've just come from my father's deathbed? Surely, yes. But then, I've come to talk to him about the death of *his* father. He still lives in a world in which he's planning to be the guy whose father has died. And here am I, telling him, actually, no, I'm the guy whose father has died.

I'm the guy.

The Bridge

The train leaves the station, and pretty soon we're on the bridge – the bridge that starts in Denmark and ends in Sweden. There's a point in the middle when you're in both, or neither, and it must be true that, when you reach this point, you're simultaneously in both *and* neither.

One thing about the bridge, by the way, is that you can't really see it when you're on it.

The train leaves the station, and we're on the track, the *spor* as they say here, as in the spoor, which means footprint, and pretty soon we're on the bridge, the *bro*, which actually means log, I think – if I'd gone to see him any time in the last ten years, my father that is, I could have asked him about this, and he'd have told me to wait a moment, and he'd have gone up the stairs, the *trappe*, in Danish, or the *Treppe*, in German, which might be where we get the word trapdoor, usually a door at the top of a staircase, and he'd have reappeared with an A4 wallet file, and inside this file would be his home-made files, maybe six of them, and inside one of these files would be several pieces of paper, covered with tiny handwriting, on the subject of how the ancient word for log, used by settlers in some godless windswept part of Europe, developed into the word for bridge, becoming *brig* and *Brücke* and *bro*.

He was breathing in, and I stood up, I'm thinking. I let go of his hand, I'm thinking. He was breathing in, and I let go of his hand. Then I squeezed his shoulder. Somewhere between a tap and a squeeze. Then I stood up.

I'm on the bridge, and I'm staring at the water. What Guy Deutscher says is: the water appears to be blue. Yes – but is it blue? Is it blue because *other people* think it's blue?

I'm going across the bridge. I'm in Denmark. Before I get to Sweden, I'll be in both Denmark *and* Sweden, and I'll simultaneously be in neither Denmark *nor* Sweden. For an infinitesimally small moment, I will be everywhere and nowhere.

But that can't be true.

When I saw those bodies that time. In the eighties. I went home. The next day I sat on my bed the whole day. My mind was blank the whole day.

My father picked me up at the station. He knew. He knew that something was wrong.

Now, on the bridge, my mind keeps going blank. But—

In the ward, I knew that something was wrong. He breathed in. I let go of his hand. I let him go. I stood up. Started to walk. Took one step, and then another.

Outside it was black. Inside it was warm. The ward at the end of the line. The ward, the place of wardens, where they guard you. The guardians, the masters of ceremony, masters of the curtains.

Why this ceremony, asks Karl Ove. When somebody dies, why do we rush to cover up their body? In hospitals, he says, bodies are taken to special rooms via special routes, and they exit the hospital from special exits, and they are borne from these special exits by special vehicles – vehicles without windows. Then they are taken to special buildings, where they are hidden as close to the ground as possible. And we know what happens next – they are shut in boxes, which are burned or buried. In our society, we must keep dead bodies out of sight.

But what, asks Karl Ove, is being repressed?

What?

I let my father go, took one step, and then another. Was this a sort of primal revenge, for thrusting me back at my mother when I was a baby? Cogs already turning in my baby brain. You think this is OK – to *thrust* me? Well, I'm not going to forget this. One day, when you're as vulnerable as I am now, I might just *thrust* you. But who will I be thrusting you towards? St Peter? If you're lucky. And if you're not so lucky, then who? Old Nick, that's who.

But no. I don't think it was a primal revenge. Because newborn babies don't have functional memories. And because, when I started to walk away, I did not think he'd just taken his final breath. But then, I did know it was *one* of his final breaths. Dr Khan would say: how many more breaths did you think he had in him?

I'd say, OK, maybe a few.

A few?

Twenty?

Come *on*.

Five?

That's more like it. At best.

So I was leaving him. To die alone. But—

But it was not premeditated. It was an impulse. I was sitting on a plastic chair, in the ward at the end of the line. Outside it was black. Inside it was warm. I knew he was dying. I didn't want to be with him when he died. But I did want to be with him when he died. I was entering a state of shock. A panic state. I did not want, but I did want, but I did not, but I did.

He breathed in. It was his last breath. His final breath. I let him go. I took one step. Two steps. Now I was level with the end of the bed. The top half of him was propped up. The bottom half was swathed in a blanket. Did they have some kind of system? I wondered. Because—

Then there was the noise. I won't say much about the noise. But sometimes it's described as a rattle. This is the final breath being expelled. But not in the same way as the penultimate breath was expelled, and all the breaths prior to that, muscles in the diaphragm and neck taking their cue from a signal originating in the medulla. The final breath is different. The final breath is a bubble of carbon dioxide being forced out of the oral and nasal passages under pressure.

I'm trying to get this clear in my memory. I'm at the end of the bed. Then: the rattle. Then I look at my father's face. Willing him to take one more breath. Just one more would do it. One more breath and I could go back to the plastic chair and hold his hand as if nothing had happened. But he won't take one more breath, and I know this.

I find a nurse. The nurse is a few feet away. And I say something to the nurse.

What I say is a lie.

And by the way, you might be wondering about the nurse. She's the one with the clipboard. Why didn't the nurse know exactly what was going on? Why didn't she hear the final breath? The forcing of the bubble of gas under pressure from the nasal and oral passages. Why did she not hear this?

Because, at this exact moment, the ward at the end of the line is noisy. It's like a cocktail party. Eight beds, eight very old men. Some visitors. Several people talking at once. Trays and containers, beakers and cans of drink, knives and forks, all tapping and sliding and hissing. Pipes and vents, as befits an elaborate heating and air-conditioning system. Beeping and chirping from the nurses' station along the corridor. Muffled voices. Flushing noises from the plumbing. Some groans. Possibly some snores. The insect buzz emanating from headphones. Traffic noise from outside.

I walk towards the nurse. Just a few steps. She turns round. But I can't tell her what I've just seen – and what

I've just heard. So I tell her something else. I say I think my father looks uncomfortable. I say I think he looks like he may be in trouble. I'm sorry to bother her, I say, I know she's busy, but anyway.

She looks at me. She will check. She asks me to wait in the corridor while she checks.

This is what I'm thinking as the train crosses the bridge, as I change trains, as I move across the southern tip of Sweden towards Ystad, where I will meet Karl Ove. I don't want to think that I abandoned my father at the exact moment of his death. But I think I did.

I get off the train at Ystad. Karl Ove is very friendly. We get into his van. His van is very untidy, which makes me like him. Soon we are driving along a country road edged with mounds of snow and ice. We make small talk.

'Um,' I say.

Then: 'Um, I know I've come to talk to you about the death of your father, but . . . my father died. Literally. I was at his deathbed.'

I look at Karl Ove. He is looking at the road.

'Like, yesterday,' I say.

The Peace Process

Over the next few days I try to piece together certain strange things that happened in the ward at the end of the line.

My memory gets to work.

So: go back to the crucial moment. I notice something about my father. I get the attention of the nurse. Sorry to bother you, I say, but I think my father may be in trouble. That's the expression I use – 'in trouble'. Like he's a schoolboy, and I have come to collect him, wearing a deerstalker hat. He's been drinking too much, sniffing glue, spreading lies about matron.

Sorry to bother you, I say to the nurse, but I think my father is in trouble.

She tells me to go and wait in the corridor. Soon after this – very soon, a few moments – another nurse is walking towards me, and then she stops. She tells me, in a gentle voice, that she's sorry to say that my father has died.

I say: 'Yes, yes, I think you're right.' Now I feel a very strong urge – I want to check, to make sure that my father *has* died. Partly because this nurse – well, how can she know for sure? At this point, I think my father is probably dead, is almost certainly dead – but possibly not. After all, it was me who told the nurse! It was my idea! And now this other nurse is just repeating the thing I said, which I'm now regretting having said.

When I get to his bed, they have drawn the curtains – already! Just like they did with Mr Barely Alive – who is still lying there, mouth open, eyes closed, still barely alive. They thought *he* was dead. But then he started shouting. And you don't shout after you die, do you? Your hair might keep on growing for a few minutes, whatever. But you don't shout, do you?

I say: 'Look, do you mind if I just—' I don't say the word 'check'. I don't say, look, I know you think you're experts at telling dead people apart from living people, but so far, in my experience, you haven't always been right, have you?

I don't say *that*.

I open the curtains. A tiny part of me expects my father to be looking like he's possibly alive. Maybe he's sitting up in bed, drinking a cup of tea and eating a biscuit, waiting for me to come and collect him in a taxi.

But he looks more dead than I've ever seen him. He is supine and unmoving. I place my fingertips on his forehead. His eyes are closed. He is not even trying to breathe. He is no longer fighting death, no longer fighting the waves of microbes, as they eat him from the inside. He looks upsettingly peaceful. At peace, as they say – because life, if you think about it, is war. Death is peace. I understand this now. Peace stinks. That's why people love war so much. Because it makes them feel alive.

I start to talk to him. Just in case. Just in case of the anaerobic brainwaves.

'Anyway,' I say.

And: 'I've just been talking to the nurses.'

And: 'And they think—'

I find myself standing over my father's body, his remains, what's left of him – or, as Karl Ove might say, the part of him that has 'entered the world of death'.

I haven't planned anything. I just blurt out what's on my mind. I start telling him, in an apologetic tone, that I have some bad news, that the nurses have told me – I try to give him the impression that this is not me, not my opinion, but strictly the opinion of the nurses . . . the thing is, I say, they think you have died.

'*But*,' I say, 'I'll still chat to you. For a while.'

Standing above him, or rather the material that might be him in the act of becoming his body, the warring flesh as it capitulates to the peace process, I try to sum up the last few hours of what I've been saying – that I love him (true); that he's been a good father (untrue); that he's inspired me (true, but tricky); that I'll miss him (true, although this is complicated); that we'll all miss him (true, I think); that I'll miss his love of words (true); that I won't forget him (true). And more. A speech is emanating from me, and I think it's hitting the right note, and this does not occur to me at the time, but the note I'm hitting – somehow, by some miracle of language – is keeping him alive for me. Not fully. Not really. Almost not at all.

But the curtains are closed. It's just me and him now. And science says the brain still lives for a while. The anaerobic brainwaves. The eels—

So here we are. Father and son. Chatting away.

Then I say goodbye. A very emotional moment. For me, certainly. For him? I don't know. Perhaps the whole thing, the whole dying thing, is very emotional. I bet it is. Maybe it consists of pure emotion, unalloyed by reason. Maybe there's a moment when the brain, in its final squishy, wobbling moment, contrives a dream-like spectacle of the dying person's life, painted in the colours of pure emotion. Who knows?

'Well,' I say. 'Goodbye then. And . . . thanks.'

The moment I step outside the curtains, and back into the ward, I want to go back inside the curtains. But I don't. The nurses are here. So I walk out of the ward, and along the corridor as far as the half-wall behind which Mr Ninety-Nine lives. At the moment, he's in bed, eyes closed, definitely alive, hair still sticking up in his nonagenarian's quiff.

I compose myself. In the stairwell I call my mother, who answers quickly. I'm not sure what to say.

'I'm terribly sorry to say this, but—'

'Has he died?'

'Well, as I say, I'm sorry to say this.'

She says: 'Darling!'

Not to me. To my father.

She cries. She asks me various questions. Yes, I was there. Yes, it was peaceful.

After we hang up I'm gripped with a horrible thought. What if my father is not actually dead. What if he has not died? I've just been talking to him. I've just been talking to him in the hope that he might still be alive.

And now it seems I've done the cruellest thing. I have said the thing that might have been designed to hurt my mother the most. What if it's a lie!

I have told her he's dead – when he might still be alive! Now she thinks he's dead.

I need to make sure he's dead. I need to go behind the curtains again.

Half a minute later I'm back in the ward. Just before he took his last breath, a long time ago, I was desperate to get out of here. Now you couldn't keep me away.

I find the nurse.

'Look, is there anything . . . like, do I have to sign something?'

'No. Don't worry.'

'Because, when somebody dies . . .'

'No. You don't need to do anything else.'

'But. Now he's dead, right . . . I mean, he's dead, yes?'

'You can go home now.'

'Yes. But when somebody dies – I mean. He's dead.'

The nurse looks at me. I look at the nurse.

'He's dead.'

She says nothing. I say: 'Let me just – see him one more time.'

Behind the curtains, my father is still there. Still the same. Still dead. Definitely dead. I leave. I know I must not come back. My father must be taken, via secret routes, to secret places.

I walk out of the ward, out of the hospital, across the road.

At the taxi rank, I get into the first taxi.

'My father just died,' I say. 'I mean literally.'

Numb

Days later I am still numb – numb with a creeping sense of things not being quite right. I get through the day. Every few minutes I remember. My father. Of course. I don't exactly miss him. We were never close. But there is something I do miss. I miss the fact of him being alive.

I miss the possibility that, at some point, we might become close.

In my parents' house, which is now my mother's house, people keep telling me how good it was that I was with my father at the very end. After a while, my memory fixes this for me. My memory tells me that, far from abandoning my father at the end, I was with him at the end – even after the end.

I'm the guy who stayed. Which is a lie. And then, after a while, less of a lie.

My brother and I visit my mother every day. We're supposed to be organising the funeral. But I'm not doing anything. It's all him. Coffin, church, crematorium, wake. I tell him I don't want to go and see the body. Nor does he. Seeing the body might tip me over the edge, and my brain is scrambled enough already.

In my mother's house, people come and go. They have tea and cake. We look at photographs. When we do this, the narrative of my father is gently tweaked. The shape of our lives becomes smoother, the strange decisions he made more logical.

'Here's a picture of the boys in Canada when they were little. You loved the snow, didn't you?'

'Yes,' I say. 'We both loved the snow. I remember we'd listen to the radio in the morning, when they listed all the schools that were closed because of the snow. I kept listening for the name of our school. It always came near the end.'

'St Michael and All Angels.'

'Yes, that's right. St Michael and All Angels.'

'Oh, and where's this? I think it must be Freiberg.'

'Let me see,' I say, looking at the shiny square. 'Actually, it's Heidelberg.'

'That's where we went to that Mozart concert,' says my mother. 'Where they played on ancient instruments. And that fat woman appeared out of nowhere and put her arms around your father.'

I hand the photograph back. My brother has been arranging them in separate boxes.

'Do you remember that fat woman?'

I say, 'Um, I *think* . . . think so.'

Elderly ladies arrive, and sit on the sofa, and drink tea, and eat cake.

My mother says: 'We keep finding things. A postcard from Alaska in 1973. A hotel bill from Ceylon in 1970.'

One old lady says: 'It was all a bit hush-hush, I should think.'

I say: 'No! He was really just . . . going to see psychologists. So they could, you know. Share their ... results.'

My mother says: 'I remember when he went to that place in Ceylon. He wasn't back for weeks. He said he had to go somewhere in India.'

'Oh, look at this.'

It's a picture of me in Paris, in my teens, and I remember how I felt at that exact moment. A few days before I'd found a book of my father's, the Royal Canadian Air Force Exercise Plan – a book he never used. Of course he never used it! I used it just once. For five minutes. You had to do this jumping thing. I landed on the side of my foot and something cracked. It was the fifth metatarsal on my left foot – a greenstick fracture, they said at the hospital. I didn't need treatment. Just a bandage and a couple of weeks of rest. But we were just about to go to Paris to meet my father. That's pretty much what we did – met him. He was busy, anyway. I don't think in the whole time he had the slightest idea I'd hurt my foot.

'Yes,' I say. In the picture I'm smiling. The feeling in the foot was a combination of dull and sharp pain. I've had mild complications ever since. (Knee, ankle.)

Looking at the picture unlocks a specific emotion. At the time I was worried about everything. My marks at school, my poorish reports, my inability to speak French fluently, my tennis game, my weight, the fact that I was falling behind in maths, my parents' forthcoming move to Canada, boarding school, girls, the pain in my left foot, Latin, spots, my arm muscles. In comparison, my father seemed so certain about everything. Dashing around in a pale summer jacket. Never around for long. Always in a hurry.

In my mother's house, the people come and go. Old ladies on their own, or in twos, or the old-lady-with-older-man combination, of which the man is always the quieter.

My brother sits at the dining table, sorting through the photographs. He will put them in albums. He will make them into books.

My mother says, of my father: 'He was picking blackberries and he fell into a bush. And his leg got stuck in the brambles. And then this man – he was Japanese – this man just yanked him out. His leg was bleeding. That was the start of it.'

'But that cut healed, Mum.'

'It didn't. Not really.'

I sit on the sofa. I'm numb. Things don't feel quite right. But I don't want to cry.

The Tape

I listen to the tape of my interview with Karl Ove Knausgaard. On the tape, fifteen hours after my father's death, I am calm, much too calm; I have just been riding along in Karl Ove's van, which was messy in a way that made me like him, and when I was in the van I burbled something about how I was sorry to have to say this, on account of the fact that he is the guy whose father has died, but no, I said, I'm the guy – or rather that is effectively what I said, and at the moment of switching the tape on, having arrived at his house, I'm not sure if he heard what I said, or understood it. There was traffic noise, plus noise from the van's engine.

On the tape I am calm. Just two hours ago, on the bridge, I was crazed – from an old Germanic word meaning cracks in something that has been glazed, i.e. ceramics. Think of *crazy paving* from the seventies. You smash the paving stones into random shapes, and then put them back together. Crazed, cracked. Think of the French word *écraser* – to crush.

But on the tape I am calm – really, much too calm when you think I've told him what I've just told him. At the time of the tape, he probably thinks I was joking. A sick joke. In the van. Just to kick things off. Hey – my father is dead, too. Literally, dude. He probably filed this away, as possibly misheard, or worse – possibly a sicko.

On the tape, Karl Ove and I are sitting in his house, which is actually three houses, three sides of a courtyard – one house he lives in with his family, another a guest house, and there's a third in which he works, smokes and keeps his library. And his drum kit. All three houses are bungalows. The one we're in is beautifully Scandi-simple, with I suppose Quaker-like furniture, simple and elegant, and a colour scheme in pale tones of grey and blue, perfect for the Baltic light. His wife, Linda, is not here. She's in hospital, about to give birth to her and Karl Ove's fourth child. Theoretically, he could get a call any time.

He has bought us, presumably on the way back from the hospital, some sandwiches – beef with strong pickles in proper bread, very chewy, it might play havoc with my dental work. He asks me if I'm a vegetarian. No, I tell him. Then, for some reason, I say: 'I *was*.' Which sounds odd and sinister, to go along with the odd, sinister thing I said, or think I said, in the van.

But on the tape I am *so calm.* Controlled, focused. Focused on the fact that I've come to Sweden to talk about the death of Karl Ove's father, not mine. Although it's at this point that I make a decision to say, look, my father really did die yesterday – what I said in the van was true. I will say this, or something like it, is what I'm thinking. But I won't just blurt it out. I will wait for the right time.

For a while, on the tape, what you hear is chewing. We are eating the beef and pickle sandwiches. I say: 'Mmm.' He asks me if I've been to Sweden before. I tell him about the four times I've been to Sweden. Once when I met some fascists. Once to write about IKEA. Et cetera. Pretty soon we're talking about Scandinavian languages – he's trilingual in Swedish, Norwegian and Danish – and I find myself explaining how the Norwegian word for snake comes from the Old German *slange*, whereas the Swedish word for snake comes from the Norse *orm*, which is like worm; I'm reliving an actual conversation I had with my father.

Listening to this, I can only conclude that, for long periods of the two-hour conversation, I made myself forget about the events of the day before, simply put them out of my mind. On the tape I am not quite my normal self. I am a detail-hunter, wanting to pick the bones out of everything.

He tells me about his father's death, which happened during a period when he, Karl Ove, was having a terrible crisis. He was married. He'd been unfaithful to his wife. A man had called his flat, accusing him, falsely, of rape. His marriage began to unravel. He went to live on a tiny island, where he drank and felt suicidal. Around this time his father, who had been drinking himself to death, died. On the tape, Karl Ove says he wanted to write about his father's death, but couldn't do it for ten years.

At the end, as I'm preparing to leave, I say: 'It's been such an extraordinary day for me . . . I mean, my mother said, she was so upset . . . and I woke up this morning with this appalling thought, that this was not real. And there's a part of me that still doesn't believe what's happened.'

There is a silence, and I say: 'But I told people on the phone what happened. A bit like when you leave the house and you think: did I switch this off? And you know you switched it off.'

I'm not making sense.

I say: 'It's obviously shock.'

Karl Ove says: 'Mm. Yes.'

Crazy – yes, he's probably thinking. Sicko – maybe not, he's probably thinking. He tells me he'll drive me to the station.

The tape ends, and after this we walk across the frosted courtyard towards the van.

A Day Out

Life won't get back to normal until after the funeral, I keep telling myself. In the meantime, I do lots of things that don't seem quite normal. I take my son skateboarding. I take him to the shops. I don't communicate with his mother, beyond accepting her commiserations, because we are still estranged. Everything I do, or don't do, takes place in a world in which the air smells different. The air smells of my father's death.

When my father's father died, I accompanied my father to the funeral. He had flown across from Canada because I was in trouble, and stayed around because his father was ill. He made one of his rare visits to see his parents. When he got there his mother was sitting on the sofa; her leg was in plaster after an operation. He found his father in a waking dream, rummaging through a Victorian chest of drawers. Three weeks later, my grandfather was in hospital; a week after that, he was dead.

My grandfather rummaged. Twenty-eight days later he took his final breath. My father rummaged. I count the days, from rummaging to death.

Jesus.

My father didn't seem particularly worried when his father died. There was very little fuss. My grandmother decided not to go to the funeral because of her leg. It was just me and my father, and two people we'd never met before.

When we arrived at the church, there was nobody around. We thought it was the wrong church. But it wasn't. Eventually we found the verger and asked him what was happening.

'Not again,' he said.

The vicar had got his dates mixed up. But the verger called the funeral home, and found an emergency vicar.

My father and I waited around for a couple of hours with the two people we didn't know. They were a couple in their forties. My father was in a generally upbeat mood. I remember the way he charmed the couple. Then the emergency vicar arrived. The funeral people came with the coffin. The emergency vicar performed a very short service. Later, we went to the crematorium.

When I remember this day my mind gives me images of the small church, of the way the gravestones looked in the light, of the couple in their forties sitting on a wooden bench. The mood evoked is light-hearted – a day out that went wrong, but that was salvaged in the end. My father and I both wore grey suits. I was seventeen. He was fifty. I hadn't felt so close to him in ages.

The Start of Something

On the day of my father's funeral I get up early, drink a cup of coffee, have a shower and walk around my bedroom in a towel while I choose my clothes. A grey suit – definitely. I try it with different shirts. A black one. A black one with a white motif, the exact shirt Mel Gibson was wearing when he was arrested for drink driving, I'm pretty sure. I've also got another one, black with tiny polka dots.

I trimmed the stubble on my face before I stepped in the shower. The funeral will be in the church across the village green from my parents' street. We will file into the church. I will sit in the front row. Some people will bring the coffin. My brother has arranged everything. He will read a eulogy.

My hair doesn't look too bad. I will brush it back, using a tiny bit of wax. The trick is to do this an hour in advance – this way, if you use too much wax, you can rewash your hair and start all over again. My father lost a little bit of his hair in his twenties – it receded at the temples. But he didn't lose much more after that. His father didn't lose any hair at all.

I'll be looking at the coffin, knowing his body's in there. His body. In the coffin. Because we have to cover up the dead. Karl Ove asks: why? It's a good question. I might be crazy, but I'm not a sicko, is another thing he probably thinks, if he ever thinks of me. How was your day, Karl Ove? Well, this guy came to interview me. Oh, how was he? Well, he was crazy. But not a sicko.

I try the shirt with tiny black polka dots, Agnès B, and a black tie, with the grey suit. The truth is, it's not actually a suit. I spent a while looking for a pair of trousers in the jacket's exact shade of grey. Nobody would know. I can wear black suede shoes.

The outfit works, and now I feel terrible because my son's mother, who is not coming to the funeral, won't see me like this. My son is also not coming to the funeral, on the grounds that he's too young. He'll go to school as usual.

I can't eat breakfast but I'm going to walk around the town for a while and get a taxi to my parents' house. I don't want to go to a funeral today. I don't want to go to my father's funeral today. What if he hadn't got up that night? What if he hadn't made a noise – did he crash into something? – and decided to sit at the bottom of the stairs? What if his kidneys hadn't failed? What was under that blanket? Some sort of system, they must have had some sort of system.

If the kidneys had failed, they wouldn't be making urine. So where did all the water go?

What water?

Nobody gave him any water.

Did we just forget?

I walk down the path and into the street and into town, walking with purpose, with my stubble trimmed, with my slightly waxed hair brushed back, my grey suit, nobody would know it isn't a suit, and the shirt with black polka dots, which is one notch more cheerful than you'd expect a shirt to be at a funeral, contrasting with the black tie – sombre, meaning shadowy, connected to the Italian *umbra*, and the Spanish *sombra*, so you get umbrella and sombrero.

I'm walking along, thinking about the water. Maybe we just forgot to give him any water. Nobody told me to give him water. Maybe it's one of those things, like when you're looking after somebody's cat, and you just forget—

And there she is!

At first I think I must be imagining it – that it's a hallucination. My son's mother. But it's not a hallucination. It's her. She sees me. I see her. I walk towards her.

'Hi.'

'Hi.'

For a few moments, we look at each other. She sees me. The hair. The stubble. The shirt. The tie. Slightly more cheerful. Slightly more sombre. I see her. She looks beautiful. Something passes between us and I know we won't be estranged for ever.

In the church I'm jittery. People bring in the coffin. The coffin people. They bring it here, they will take it to the crematorium. The vicar stands on a podium behind a bronze eagle. When I was in my atheist teens I used to come in here, not alone, and stand on the podium behind the bronze eagle and make speeches.

Now my brother stands on the podium. I can see the angle of the finger I snapped. He says what a great man our father was, how we travelled around with him, how we loved him, how I was with him until the very end. I can sense people looking at me, but I don't lift my head. I think of myself getting up, taking the two steps, hearing the rattle. Then talking to the nurse. I told them he was dead. They told me he was dead. I told him he was dead. His brain activity by now anaerobic. I came back. Got behind the curtains. Carried on talking. There are still holes in my story.

At the crematorium, we wait in the anteroom. There's a coffee machine you don't have to pay for. There's a big chimney, for when they burn the bodies. We file in. It's just me and my brother and my mother. It occurs to me I'll need to change the setting on my phone that says 'Parents'.

The coffin is in place. One of the coffin people says a few words. I'd planned to think my most positive thoughts about my father at this moment. So I do. I think of us driving by the lake. I think of the chowder hut. I think of how I felt as he drove me to the airport in the Ford, how I felt we could talk about anything now. As the organ music starts up, as the coffin moves towards the curtains, and then beyond the curtains, I think about the moment in the airport when I reached the barrier, it all happened so soon, and I looked behind me, and there he was, and I looked behind me again, and he'd gone, and I walked across the tarmac, into the snow, thinking yes, this was the start of something.

Acknowledgements

Let's start with my brother, Alex Leith. In the book, I've given the impression that Alex is the guy I tormented when we were children, and who has been angry with me ever since. All true. As his older brother, I did torment him. I should not have done that. Sometimes I can feel my brain telling me that maybe it wasn't too bad, wasn't my fault. But it was. And it was.

What I really want to say is that Alex is not just this angry person – to everybody else, he's charming, funny and gregarious. I don't know anybody who has more friends than Alex. Next to Alex, *I'm* the toxic one. Writing memoirs makes people more one-dimensional than they actually are, because you can only see them as they relate to you. Anyway, maybe we can be friends now – or sometime in the future.

Thanks, Alex.

I'd also like to thank my parents. Yes, including my father! I know he was largely absent from my life, but his absence and occasional presence helped to define me. And I loved him. Also my mother. She bore it all with dignity: the countless trips to strange places, the burden of trying to make it all seem normal. Thanks for that.

Thanks also to my agent Antony Topping, my editor Michael Fishwick, my copyeditor Robert Davies, and managing editor Lauren Whybrow. Thanks also to Harriet Green, then at the *Guardian*, now the *Observer*, for publishing the original piece that led to this book. Thanks to my early readers – Dodie Horton, Jonathan Waters, Callum Murray, Alex Leith, Miriam Darlington. And thanks to Susan for all the support.

A Note on the Type

The text of this book is set Adobe Garamond. It is one of several versions of Garamond based on the designs of Claude Garamond. It is thought that Garamond based his font on Bembo, cut in 1495 by Francesco Griffo in collaboration with the Italian printer Aldus Manutius. Garamond types were first used in books printed in Paris around 1532. Many of the present-day versions of this type are based on the *Typi Academiae* of Jean Jannon cut in Sedan in 1615.

Claude Garamond was born in Paris in 1480. He learned how to cut type from his father and by the age of fifteen he was able to fashion steel punches the size of a pica with great precision. At the age of sixty he was commissioned by King Francis I to design a Greek alphabet, and for this he was given the honourable title of royal type founder. He died in 1561.